Window of Self,

A Diary is Forever

Instructions, techniques and history for the diary writer.

By

Raymond Lee Zager

Published by

The Diary Library of Corralitos

330 Eureka Canyon Road

Corralitos, CA 95076, USA

Library of Congress Cataloguing in Publication Data

Raymond Lee Zager 1924-present.

Window of Self, A Diary is Forever.

ISBN 0-9742395-0-X

Printed in the United States of America on acid-free paper

First printing

Introduction

Window of Self, A Diary is Forever is a comprehensive book about diary writing. It is intended for a wide audience.

Thousands of people keep diaries; diary writing popularity has been steadily growing since the 1970's. In one volume, *Window of Self, A Diary is Forever,* combines many aspects of diary writing experiences, offering numerous instructional techniques, examples of diary writing (including the author's own "Dialogues"), an historical look at various diarists and a list of published diaries, and (for future study and travel) a list of diarists sites (such as The Pepys Library in England), many of which are Historical Landmarks.

The title, *Window of Self*, points to the fact that diarists can't help but reveal who they are as they record their personal interests, relationships, activities, state of mind and what is happening that day. The subtitle, *A Diary is Forever*, reminds the reader that, except for carelessness, acts of god or intentional destruction, a diary becomes a permanent record of an individual's life and is thus "forever."

Window of Self, A Diary is Forever, has something to offer everyone who has an interest in learning about the diary genre. It is an invaluable book for the beginning diarist, and an important resource and guide for those who already write, read, or study diaries and journals.

It is the author's aim to fire up the enthusiasm of the reader as to the value of the diary. Value, as shown by examples from great writers. One such value, is keeping information through recordation. It's to be used by the diarist and those that follow. Each of us has the opportunity to record, not just Emerson, Nin or Pepys. Not only the conscious happenings, but also our unconscious out-croppings can be recorded and be given whatever merit it deserves.

As humans, our memories are fallible. We forget at every chance. Most of us make lists of foods before we go to the grocer. A diarist has a third memory; it's his diary. He can always go back and find the information there.

What does the diarist put in his diary? There are too many items or ideas to mention; yet, here are a few. John Muir experimented with the body of a grasshopper; he used it as a stamp (ink stamp pad) and then made a border to his page. A lot of us just write facts with no accompanying feelings. Novelists usually play with plots and words in theirs. Poets capture thoughts, pictures and ideas. Naturalists abound in nature, a la Thoreau and Burroughs.

Shouldn't the diary be organized? Yes! To help in this regard an entire chapter is devoted to it. It includes a reward for returning the diary book, dedications (to set a tone), the last page (a summary) and an index.

There are four chapters on getting the unconscious on to the pages of the diary book. These are Meditation, Dreams (night), Dialogues and Hypnogogic Imagery. Because these chapters will allow ideas, pictures, scenes and stories to come to conscious mind, these chapters are valuable to all who want to use them. Thomas Edison used hypnogogic imagery to find matters of science, and Edgar Allen Poe for his stories. Poets and writers have dwelt in these halls. Everyone and anyone can use these ideas and procedures and record them in their diary. Inventions, how to improve the world, stories, poetry and visions can come during the alpha and alpha-beta brain wave state.

Landmarks and sites for diarists chapter was written in commemoration of those famous diarists we still celebrate. It tells the world who they are (a short biography for each) and then locates the site for you to visit.

The last chapter "Published Dairy Books," is for those who want to do further study in the field.

About the Author

Raymond Lee Zager is a retired lawyer and a devoted diarist. He has been teaching diary writing since the 1970's, and has given classes in Los Angeles, and in Santa Cruz at Dominican Hospital and the University of California. He has been collecting published diary books since 1976 and owns the second largest diary library in the United States; his Special Collections of children's diaries, Concord (Massachusetts) diaries and the diaries of Samuel Pepys have been exhibited in libraries in California. He has written articles concerning diaries for the *Diarist's Journal* magazine and he has been interviewed on radio stations about his diary library and his published memoir *Private Zager, 71st Infantry Division.* He continues to write his own diary, which now consists of 78 volumes. He lives with his wife, Helen, in Santa Cruz, California, and has five children and seven grandchildren.

Acknowledgements

To all those who helped in the writing of this book, I must personally thank all of you.

To my dear wife Helen, without her the book would not be. She has been at my side as I gathered the facts, theories and concepts for this book. Twenty-six years ago until now, we talked almost daily of the diary ideas. Her judgment was prized and highly regarded. She is my biggest benefactor.

Steve Kay is my clerk extraordinaire. He and I have worked on the book for over two years. He typed the entire manuscript and put in his heart, and his counter offenses, when it counted. We talked out each aspect of the book. I value his forthright judgment and his quick response. Of course, during the time together, Steve and I have become very good friends. He is a key figure in the bridge in which the words went into the book.

Olivia Dresher of Seattle, Washington, has been a diarist most of her life. She was an academic editor with the University of Washington. We had a long talk a few years ago, when she offered to edit *Window of Self*. She wanted to help me and keep her hand in the diary field, pro bono. I said, "No, you must charge for your services." We agreed on a price. Olivia edited the entire book. She would not allow any word, comma, period or colon to escape her. Though she worked in Seattle and I in Santa Cruz, (Corralitos) we worked by correspondence and phone. She is a delightful person, has published an anthology on diarists *Darkness and Light: Private Writing as Art* and has her own diary publishing company Impassio Press. It was wonderful working with her.

Along this, the twenty-six year trail, a marathon in the collection of ideas, books, meeting people and writing a lot of it in my own diary; I want to recognize those who are important to the book.

To those in the United Kingdom: Peter Thompson, who pointed me towards Pepys' Library Cambridge, his wife Sandy (from Los Angeles) who took her children, Helen and I to meet Opal Whiteley. Robert Latham, the librarian of Pepys Library, who joined me in the celebration of diarists (Pepys, and Dorothy Wordsworth) and then helped me with the Pepys Exhibit at Beverley Hills Library. E.J.C. West, secretary to the Kilvert Society, known as the "dogs body," because he had so many jobs to do, took Helen and me within his heart, (we corresponded for years). Elizabeth Lawrence, for helping me find the whereabouts of Opal Whiteley and being a friend over the years.

To those in the United States I take pleasure in noticing them.

To my diary teachers, Dr. Frances Heussenstamm, Tristine Rainer, Lea Schweitzer, Holly Prado and Claire Braz-Valentine.

I want to thank the Dominican Hospital here in Santa Cruz, Ca, for allowing me to teach diary writing for nine years to those in the mental health ward. My same thanks to the Mental Health Client Action of Santa Cruz for allowing me to teach their members the techniques and history of diary writing.

Lastly Ed Gildea, Joe Peebles and Hollie Rose, editors in succession of the national magazine, the Diarist's Journal, I say, "Thanks," for publishing all my articles.

Table of Contents

K. Recording.   109

1. Keep it; do not let it slip away.
2. Learn the rules.
   a. Relax the body and mind.
   b. Be alert.
   c. Recognition.
   d. A place to record.
   e. Motivation.
3. A carefree vacation is fertile time.
4. Writing *Fight for Life*.
5. Meditation into twilight state.
6. Benefits.
7. Be alert.
   a. Thomas Alva Edison invented his own startle.
   b. You may have a natural startle.
8. Recognition of image.
   a. Be aware they exist and learn to recognize them.
   b. Alert at the period of their existence.
   c. Be aware just before sleep and coming out of sleep.
   d. How long do they last?
9. Appropriate setting to record.
   a. Use diary book, creates feeling of permanence.
   b. Night.
      (1) Do not turn on lights.
      (2) Eyes closed – use the squint.
      (3) Image precious – get it all down.
      (4) Only low light behind you.
      (5) Read at a later time.
   c. Day.
      (1) All light, sun and artificial to be avoided.
      (2) A shaded area to record.
      (3) Avoid distraction of people and animals.
      (4) Samuel Taylor Coleridge example.
10. Motivated to record.
    a. It has great usefulness.
    b. It's yours and no one else's. Your monopoly.

Chapter 1

The Values, Pleasures and Pain Within a Diary

The Values of Diary Writing

While teaching a diary writing class at Dominican Hospital, here in Santa Cruz, California, I was asked by one of the students, "What is the value of diary writing?" I spouted out fast and long these ideas:

- you develop and create a new memory system;
- a record of your life is at your fingertips;
- poems are found in a diary;
- within a diary, dialogues and all lists, are found;
- you can write to your alter ego and the alter ego may write back to you;
- it's a place to put your emotions, a place to talk about love or loneliness, a place to write word portraits;
- something that is exclusively yours and may last forever;
- sketches and drawings fit within a diary;
- one can forget about grammar and spelling (if you want to);
- descriptive writing is present in all diaries;

Emerson, Thoreau, Muir and other naturalists wrote of nature in their diaries. Opal Whitely, while living in the Oregon woods in about 1908, from six to eight years old, wrote about nature, people and animals. These individually became her one hundred and three characters. Her diary was published by Atlantic Monthly serially (and in book form in 1920) and made her famous the world around.

James Boswell wrote about Dr. Johnson constantly in his diary, and then wrote one of the world's greatest biographies using the diary.

Samuel Pepys hid information in his diary (between 1660 and 1669) as he wrote in an indecipherable code.

Father Junipero Serra, who helped to establish all the missions of California, kept a diary during March 28 to June 1769 while on his journey from Loreto to the San Diego area. He wrote about roses covering an entire valley, Indian squaws and his holding their babies, and finding water each evening on the surface or by digging. When he finished the journey, he sent the diary to Queen Isabella.

Professor William E. Dodd, Ambassador to Germany prior to 1939, kept a diary where he noted his meetings with high-ranking officials of Germany, Italy, France, Spain, China and other governments of the world. He gleaned day-by-day information from all sources. In his diary he writes about all the characters, ambassadors and dictators, and all are listed as principal persons of the diary from Hitler, Goering, Hess, Hull, Striecher and ninety-five others.

On November 29, 1937, he wrote to David Lloyd George, Britain's Prime Minister, warning his government against entering into a "thieves bargain with dictators." He suggested: better to go to war now rather than to surrender to them.

Dodd concluded (in his letter):
"How can England do anything after allowing Mussolini to master the Mediterranean, Ethiopia and half of Spain."
December 19, 1937 (within the diary):
"I sent a message to Roosevelt summarizing information of Japanese destroying American and English vessels in Chinese waters, even killing Americans. The Czech Ambassador, who gave me the information wanted to know what the US would do. In my message to Roosevelt I gave him my opinion: if the US and

England did not stop Japan, our people would come to realize that in a year or two what their position was. I advised a boycott. I hope my message of my opinions does not reach Hitler."

After talking to me about Dodd's diary, Jake Zeitlin – the famous Los Angeles bookseller – said: "All public servants of our government should be required to keep diaries, even in code if necessary!"

Dreams, daydreams and hypnogogic imagery all find their way into the diary.

By keeping diaries, most writers save their thoughts, ideas and dreams, which can be used at another time.

Emerson wrote for many years in his diary about his concept of compensation. "Compensation" later became one of his famous essays.

Thoreau's greatest gift to mankind is not *Walden*, or his *River* writings; it is his diary, in excess of two million words. We can read his daily thoughts, and witness his remarkable mind.

Of course, even if you've written just one volume, or less than one volume, all kinds of events have happened. First, you've recorded a present event that immediately becomes history. When Mary Boykin Chesnut wrote about her husband being in Jefferson Davis' cabinet in the Civil War, it was new. Yet now, one hundred and forty one years later, it turns out to be one of the best firsthand reports of the Civil War. What you write today is new and may be valuable now, as well as later.

Human beings have conscious memories and unconscious memories. The unconscious memory is hard to get to. It comes out in dreams and other ways, thus we mainly use our conscious memory. There is a third memory; it is the diary. When you record what is important to you each day or almost each day in your diary, then the diary becomes your third memory. When you need information, it is there.

Emotions find their way into the diary. It's a very good place to write about love and loneliness; it's a place for happiness and depression. Most diaries are not shown to others. Hence, you are free to express your emotions. Samuel Pepys of England, one of the worlds' great diarists (his diaries were written from 1660 to 1669) wrote his diary completely in code. He had total freedom to write; all the King's men could not break the code. He was totally protected. His emotions were kept secret for one hundred years.

While most diarists keep a diary for themselves only, others write theirs for a child or children, or for grandchildren, to pass personal history down the limbs of the family tree. Once you've written maybe 50 pages, or perhaps a volume, feelings of ownership about your diary, as well as its value, become quite apparent. You and your family will prize it over almost any other property. It is all you – your handwriting, your thoughts, your intelligence, your use of language and how you see the world. You and your family will want to keep it safe and from harm.

I have taken extreme care to protect my diaries. I purchased a fireproof filing cabinet, which offers protection to 1700 degrees Fahrenheit. Then I learned that if you press the volumes together, not letting oxygen get to the volumes (even above the 1700 degrees), they probably won't burn.

Find a place or places in your residence where your diaries will be safe from fire, flood, animals and other dangers.

Pleasures of Diary Writing

One of the pleasures of diary writing is to record night dreams. The real pleasure is not necessarily writing down what your unconscious says, but being the detective and finding out what the dream means. Within the twilight state it seems to be quite easy, and the next day the pleasure remains even in bright daylight. The twilight state is that time or state of mind when close to sleep. It happens when you are tired and drowsy before or after sleep. Probably the best twilight state is just after awakening from a nap, or sleep, especially when it's dark and your eyes are still closed.

I wrote this many years ago:

"Running, running all day. Only driving to and from the law office, was I with "me." Yet driving in traffic or a winding road is not "me time." "Me time," is quiet, solitude in meditation, or resting, or in guided imagery, or writing to oneself, diary work. It nourishes my soul; it is what calms me; it is what I need everyday. During the day, I had contracts to pound out, I had to see a sick friend and cheer him up. Now at last, alone, with time to unwind, to have my mind relax and to say, "Hello," to me, to warrant me, to muse me, to suckle at solitude's breast."

In the diary, you will be able to find out where your pleasures are. For example, in May of 2001, while having an iced coffee at a local coffeehouse, I wrote this in my diary:

"I have a good feeling within me, that's hard to describe, it's like seeing a young child at play or myself as a child in the water at the beach. I'm sure this is the kind of feeling my readers and students may have, I hope they do. My writing or talking may not achieve this atmosphere. It may take a lot more. A good family, home, ethics…

"Still in the coffee shop, I pick up a publication for public school teachers in the West, which included Yosemite and Mariposa. This is where I want to be – in open space and at a slower pace. In a crowded city last weekend, it was a terrible place to be; it was crowded, noisy, no nature, no trees, no solitude.

"The question is, "When does this happiness come to me?" I believe it happens when I am relaxed. I see accomplishments of the past, now, and in the future. I feel I need several days of vacation to wind down. Yet it happened today with just a hot day, ice coffee, and reading about Mariposa."

Thus, I wrote of and about my own place of diary writing pleasures.

Another example took place in June 2001.

"'Tis summer. The air and the people are hot. Get to a shaded area. Put ice in a large glass and pour in sparkling soda. It's time to rejoice in the face of detrimental factual happenings. You do what you can; protect what you have left. Live life to its fullest extent. Being full of life is to take two swallows of the iced soda drink and think of what I have. A son, a daughter, both of whom have made themselves into wonderful people. A wife, who is loving to me and is smart, likes to work hard with ceramics and has the best judgment of anyone I know. So to life, to mine, Helen, Paul, Lynnanne, and to all that I care about and to the peoples of this planet. Amen."

The pleasures of writing may coincide with the pleasures and happiness you record on the pages of your diary.

Pain within a diary

We all enjoy writing of pleasure and especially recording it in our diary; it helps us to realize the day.

Unexciting or plain matters are just that and you may not want these in the diary. Yet these tidbits fill in the blank spaces, and seem to make the writing whole.

As humans, we are not in the same place all the time. We may have been happiest as a child, as a boy shooting marbles, or in our first, second or twentieth deep-sea fishing trip, or as a bridegroom. Then each day, week, month, there are ups and downs – in-between happiness, there's dullness, and maybe pain.

Pain can get you to write. There is power in pain. A young man leaves home for the first time; he may be in the army. He becomes homesick and is in pain (he cannot function). The Greeks had a name for it – melancholia. The same situation may happen when a person leaves home for the first time to go to college.

There is pain in other separations. The pain suffered by the whole family when a spouse leaves the marriage or when a child leaves home.

Certainly there is physical pain. From an accident, a fall, a bike injury, or from an illness. These are subjects to write about.

Psychological pain from a mental illness may be more devastating than a physical injury.

Many of those with mental illness, such as depression or schizophrenia, have become great writers. To name a few: Sylvia Plath, Virginia Woolf, Abraham Lincoln and Henry James.

Is it the pain that makes them exceptional or after or during the pain? It may be the circumstances. Lincoln was certainly depressed while writing and reading his speech at Gettysburg.

Virginia Woolf stopped writing when the mania she felt took over. She wrote before and afterwards.

Those in a low threshold of depression might write exceedingly well.

When in pain you may not care about anything. You may write more freely and openly. Poetry may come to you more easily.

You may feel pain for a loved one. You might be very close to a parent, and there might be signs that she is not well; but no one knows what is wrong. The illness takes months and finally there is a diagnosis; death is around the corner. Going through the crisis, you experience their pain and your own, and you can write it in your diary. This may help process that pain.

Love and pain often go together. Love of home, family, parents, siblings, a friend, nature and reading. Thus, if something happens to destroy any of these, then pain will invade and help fill the void.

Write it all; write the pleasures of your life and put in the pain as well. We are not all pleasure; we are whole.

Chapter 2

What Is A Diary and What Is Not?

The Oxford English Dictionary defines a diary as a "daily account of events or transactions; mainly a daily record of matters that affect the writer personally." American dictionaries generally follow this definition.

The main reason to keep a diary is to remember. If we had perfect memories, there would be no need for a diary. But our memories are fallible. We don't record everything we relive through our senses, dreams or other images. Most often notes are not taken in the moment. We make lists of what to buy at the grocery. We make notes to ourselves as reminders. If we do this daily – make notes of events and transactions, in detail, which affect us personally – then it's a diary.

To observe and note with care is to provide insurance against the gradual and inevitable collapse of our human memory.

Lies spoken under oath at the Nuremberg trials and continued in a diary, plus memoirs of being with Hitler makes exciting reading. Albert Speer, a high Nazi official, testified during the Nuremberg trials that he never knew of the existence of Germany's concentration camps. This statement was restated in his diary, and published in 1975 under the title "Spandau Diaries." German motion pictures shown on American television screens showed Speer inside a concentration camp.

Usually a diarist will not lie to himself in his own diary. Secrets from the world may be kept in this manner, especially when the writer knows the diary will be published. Speer was not allowed to write while in Spandau prison. He secretly wrote on cigarette and toilet paper and then hid these in his boot. A German orderly smuggled them out and delivered them to his wife in Berlin.

After spending twenty years in Spandau, he came home. Over 25,000 pieces of smuggled diary papers awaited him. From these he edited his diary. The diary was a best seller in Europe and in the United States.

There were just a few inmates in the prison. They were all previously high ranking Nazi officials. They were being guarded by men from France, England, Russia and the United States. These guards never caught on to Speer's smuggling act.

Sometimes lies are written into diaries. Maybe the writer believes the lie, or wants others or the world to believe him. If the pictures on television are true, then Speer's testimony is not. Speer probably saved himself more years in prison or a possible death sentence. Lies are fiction. When placed in a diary, it's still a diary.

American novelist Nathaniel Hawthorne wrote fiction within his diaries. He wanted to keep these stories short, so he wouldn't lose them from memory. Hawthorne, author of the *Scarlet Letter*, *The House of Seven Gables* and other novels, wrote stories in his diary. If one were a novelist, where else would he keep his stock and trade? He's not telling lies. It's either an expression of his imagination, half-truths, non-fiction or a combination of all. He's recording his imaginative thoughts, hypnogogic images or daydreamed stories to be looked at in a future time. These are the events of the writer's days, as they existed in his mind.

In December of 1837, Hawthorne wrote a fairy tale in his diary about chasing Echo to her hiding place. Echo is the voice of a reflection in a mirror.

Under the definition of a diary ("a daily account of events or transactions that affect the writer personally"), it's certainly arguable that fictional stories fall within this definition. These stories are events within the mind of the writer;

always in his thoughts, being turned round and round. These thoughts may take over the writer's entire day. He then confides to his diary what has been happening in his mind. "Matters that affect the writer personally" is the last part of the definition. What's more engaging than what goes on in the mind?

William Matthews, author of British Diaries, wrote that, "any true diary includes a multitask of details, thoughts, emotions, actions to be carefully pruned before writing."

Tristine Rainer, author of *The New Diary*, has stated that, "The diary is the only form of writing that encourages total freedom of expression. Because of its very private nature, it has remained immune to any formal rules of content, structure or style. As a result the diary can come closest to reproducing how people really think and how consciousness evolves."

Mr. E.J.C. West, once secretary to the Kilvert Society (an English Diary Association) wrote: "at least for England, diary is written for each day, while journals can be a longer span up to a point where the memory for close detail has diminished. After that it is memoir."

There have been many fictional books written in the diary format, but they aren't true diaries. They may contain headings with dates and place of writing (such as Thursday, Jan 1, 1803 London, England). Two books come to mind, as examples: *Bram Stoker's Dracula*, a mystery thriller and a wonderful book I'm now reading, the *Samurai's Garden* by Gail Tsukiyama.

Long-term memory put into writing is not a diary, but a memoir. Diary is written for the events of the day. Such writing is fresh; all details are there as the memory is just a few hours old. Memoirs may be good reading, yet the minute details are missing.

It has been claimed that pottery, paintings, letters and photographs are records of life and are therefore diaries. Pottery alone, although such handmade works may stay in existence for a thousand years, is not a diary unless daily writing is inscribed thereon. Paintings and pictures are not a diary; they may tell a story, but they don't do this in writing. Letters are written to someone else; a diary is written to ones self. Photographs and films may tell a story and reflect feelings. A camcorder comes the closest to being a diary as sound and language are recorded.

Sigmund Freud's "Kurzeste Chronic"

In 1929, Sigmund Freud started his personal record keeping, which lasted until his death in 1939.

He was in the habit of taking plain sheets of paper (folio sheets) and writing at the top "Kurzeste Chronic" (short chronicle), then the month and year. On top of the page may be "Sept 1929," then on the left side of the page would be the day (Wi 1/9 – Wednesday, first of September), and then his note: "Emmanuel Lowey 80 y."

Most of his jottings were in German, the remainder in English. He left Austria for England in 1939, as the Nazis were closing in. He was an atheist and a Jew.

After his death in 1939, his house in London was owned and occupied by his daughter Anna. Upon her demise, she willed the house and all the belongings to a charitable trust, to be turned into a museum. The chronicle – short cryptic notes – then became a part of the museum.

The ten years of personal note-taking would not mean much to anyone if the notes were not explained – because the notes consisted of only one, two or three words. Not only did Michael Molnar translate the notes (into English), he was in charge of what he calls the "annotations." The annotations were needed to explain the few words.

Let's look at the notes Freud made in January, 1933:

        We 4/1   Dr. May--Martin to Berlin

        Th 5/1   G Anton +

        We 1 8/1   L. Tiffany + New York

        Fr 27/1   Eitingon

        Su 29/1   Ruth flu, Hitler Reich's chancellor

        Tu 31/1   Galsworthy +; Jo Fi Kagran

Now for the annotations:

January 1933. 4/1 Dr. May, a general practitioner, wrote a letter to Freud, and later went to see him personally in Vienna. Dr. May wrote an article, which was later printed. Martin to Berlin – to see his brother.

5/1 G. Anton +: A classmate of Freud's from 1894 to 1905. The + (plus) means death or deceased.

18/1 Louis Tiffany died, heir to Tiffany & Co. fortune; their jewelry and silver store was in New York.

27/1 Eitingon's father died, and when visiting Freud, had not gotten over his grief.

29/1 Ruth Mack Brunswick had the flu, which was interfering with her analysis.

Hitler: the whole world knew this. No need for annotation.

31 /1 Death of England's novelist John Galsworthy. In Freud's book *Civilization and its Discontents*, he mentions Galsworthy's short story, "Under the Apple Tree."

The book *The Diary of Sigmund Freud* by the Freud Museum and Michael Molnar (translator and annotator) – is definitely not a diary.

The word 'diary' is defined by the Oxford English Dictionary as "a daily account of events or transactions; mainly a daily record of matters that affect the writer personally." In Webster's *Dictionary of Synonyms*, First Edition, 1951, page 13, the word 'account' is defined under account, 3, as "an oral or written *detailed* (author's emphasis), often firsthand statement."

One to four words for a daily entry does not meet the definition, as details are lacking.

What Dr. Freud was using was a calendar, a place to put notes of what would happen in the future as well as what was taking place then. It is admitted in the book's introduction that Dr. Freud would go back a few days or more and write in what had happened.

Even though those who put Dr. Freud's book together placed in the title the word 'diary', it is not really a diary. Why then, did they call it a diary? This may be one reason: Diary books have a special content, which the public will pay to read. If the title had been *Dr. Freud's Daily Calendar*, the number of purchasers would be greatly diminished.

Chapter 3

Purpose of the Diary

The main purpose of diary writing is to record, to make a record. It's for the diarist or others to read. To wait a year and then write what took place each day of that year is impossible. The diary, day-to-day writing, is a better method. Writing a little each day, 365 days a year, may be easier than trying to do it all at one time (Memoir). Diary writing is done daily, while memoirs are written after much time has passed. Memoirs signify a long-term memory, while a diary contains memory only for a day. It is like the comparison of a reservoir versus a fast fresh stream.

The diary can be used as a catchment. Emerson wrote in his first journal that he would want the entire universe to come into his diary, like a catchment. The entire world and the universe are bubbling, shaking, making magma, making news and profound ideas and solutions come about each day. New books are being published, read and discussed; friends are knocking at your door; family wants attention; babies are being born and others die. Maybe all the facts, emotions and feelings are within your grasp. Place what you want through your catchment.

To imagine a large catchment consider the following:
1. Boulder dam taking in all the water, mud, sediment, tree branches, animals and fish, letting it all go though the gate.
2. A stream fast running with fish, logs, watercress, boulder, rock and sand, absorbing sunshine.
3. A street drain taking in rainwater and whatever else comes into it.

From all that is there, open up, select and keep in what's important.

Assume you have this catchment, be it a stream, river or dam. Then the question arises, what do you do with it, how do you work with it? Going a little further, consider your day as a river. All during the day and night the river is flowing. Each minute something comes across, under or above the water, and some things are partially hidden. There's so much, though on some days so little. What you select, place in the dairy. Take in what you know is right for you. You are the selector. What is important to you will come from your sensibilities, personality, your stage in life and your maturity.

Acceleration of Time

The brain likes to be satisfied. Say you are on a trans pacific flight going to Japan, which will take many hours. You can talk to a person next to you over the noise of the plane, but that will last perhaps half an hour. You can read, sleep or dream to pass the time. I've made the trip several times. Each time I put the little table down from the seat ahead and reach for my diary bag.

When comfortable in flight, with the bag on my lap, I take out the diary book. I lean back and consider how to build a word estate; my need is to keep occupied. I have the tools.

What is my life's mission? My goal is my present work, but what about my family? What about my poetry? Where are my sketches? I am me. I am here; I am the main character. So write, think, explore, be excited and create. I am here and outside my window is Tokyo. Laughing – where did the time go?

How is the brain satisfied? While on this trip to Japan, in the coach section, squeezed between other passengers, you want the time to go by so you can get out of this plane, not be squeezed in, not hear or feel the buzz of the motors. In this case of a flight for thirteen hours, you want the brain to be occupied. Concentrating on diary writing is the best way to do this. When the brain concentrates on writing, – it doesn't notice the time passing. You're filling a need, a need to build...

An Estate in Words

One purpose of keeping a diary is the need to build an estate of words. It's not just the words but what they mean strung together. One paints with words by showing the tenor of the day. The words in the diary can live forever. You, your loved ones, even the public can read it. An example is the diary writing of the Reverend Francis Kilvert. He lived and worked in Hereford, England, near the Wye River. He wrote his diary from 1870 to 1879. He writes about hundreds of instances, one of which stands clear in my mind. He and his parishioners go on a hayride to a castle on a hill to bake potatoes, eat and drink. They dug a hole in the ground, placed the potatoes in it, built a fire, climbed to the castle, sang songs and were merry. The Reverend Kilvert diaries have been published; the entire world now has the opportunity to read them. His diary is rich from his caring for others and having an old fashioned good time, including his special observations.

The Adams Papers – that is, the diaries of John Adams and John Quincy Adams, from the American Revolution to the Napoleonic era – came to us in published form. We can read the writing, the diarist's thoughts and actions, just as they wrote it.

A young man, a painter of fine art, was drafted into the United States expeditionary force during World War I. He was drafted because he was a well-known painter. The U.S. Army needed him to paint on canvas the battle scenes. He not only painted the battle scenes; he used a diary to describe his actions and what went on about him. He also used a camera to take pictures of the battle scenes. He recorded the battles as he saw them in three different modes.

Paintings and pictures are similar to diaries; as are other works of art. Sculptures, decoupage, carving and many other working arts and crafts compare with diaries. The similarities are thought, creativity, using one's hand and so on. Some even tell stories. Probably photographs and paintings are most closely aligned to a diary. Both of these can show a range of emotions, yet the writings can describe in great depth and detail the feelings of a person. The diary in the hands of a thoughtful, loving person with the ability to write, describe, and feel (knowing pain and joy) can paint and click with words. Like other arts, the diary can be handed down to the next generation.

Major and Minor Diarists

Usually the diary is only for the writer, but not always. It's nobody else's business what the diary contains. No one looked at Henry David Thoreau's diaries until after his demise. His journals were found and dumped onto the floor of the local Concord church. Those who wanted to took one or more, read them, and returned them. The volumes of Henry David Thoreau have been published and read by thousands. Most major and minor diarists can tell a similar story. A major diarist is a person who has written a diary so outstanding that the work stands above the ordinary. The person may be famous for other reasons, for instance, Emerson, Thoreau and Hawthorne. The writing must be a contribution of ideas, concepts or other matters – a gift to the world. If a dairy is not stated (by some person, organization, editor or other authority) to be a major diary, then probably the conclusion is that it's a minor diary.

There are quite a few major diarists in my view. I would include Samuel Pepys, John Adams, John Quincy Adams, James Boswell, Ralph Waldo Emerson, Anne Frank, Nathaniel Hawthorne, Henry David Thoreau, Franz Kafka, Francis Kilvert, Anais Nin, Virginia Woolf, Fannie Burney, Dorothy Wordsworth, Katherine Mansfield, Marie Bashkirtseff, Marie Henri Beyle (Stendhal), Lewis

Carroll, Countess Sophia Tolstoy, Wanda Gag, Mary Boykin Chesnut, John Steinbeck and John Evelyn.

Most of these persons are famous and have given something special to the world. These diarists confirm my opinion and certainty that there are others who could be added to this list (see the paragraphs ahead for more comprehensive lists). I didn't include any diarists from outside the United States or Great Britain unless they have been translated into English. Since people in China (and other countries in the orient) started to write diaries several hundred years before those living in Britain, the United States and its thirteen colonies, there must be many outstanding diarists there. The same reasoning can be applied to those countries in Europe, South America and other places; that is, there are important diaries written and published in foreign languages that haven't been translated into English. Most of the collectors of diaries in the United States collect diaries in English and those that have been translated into English.

Those diarists translated into English, from my list, are: Anne Frank, Franz Kafka and Anais Nin (her first diaries were in French). Of course, hundreds – maybe thousands – more have been translated into English. A young child's diary written in Portuguese, the diary of Helen Morley, was translated by our own Elizabeth Bishop. There is the heartbreaking story of the Vilna Ghetto by Yitskhok Rudashevski – the systematic extermination of every human being in the ghetto by the Nazis. It was translated into English from the original Yiddish manuscript.

Frida Kahlo, from Mexico, wrote her diary in Spanish and it was translated into English in 1995. I have in my library a few French diaries translated into English: *The Intimate Journals of George Sand, Julian Green's Diary, Edmund and Jules De Goncourt Journals* (journals of two brothers), *A.O. Barnabooth*

Diary, Diary of an Art Dealer by Rene Ginpel, and last (but maybe the best) *Andre Gide's Journals.*

One reason why diary book collectors (of both published books and unpublished manuscripts) usually do not collect diaries in foreign languages is that they probably want to read them before they go into their collection. Most people in the United States do not read foreign language diaries, unless they have been translated. There are four diary book collectors that I know of here in the United States. James Cummings has by far the largest collection; he resides in Wisconsin. Then two ladies, Olivia Dresher of Seattle, Washington, and Hollie Rose of Middleton, Connecticut are collectors and myself. Olivia Dresher is also the curator and founder of the Library of Journals, Diaries and Notebooks located in Richard Hugo House, a literary center, in Seattle, Washington. Universities and institutions of the United States (museums) collect diaries, but I do not know if they collect non-translated foreign diaries.

Chapter 13, *Published Diary Books*, starting on page 161, includes further individual books not listed in this chapter. You can find diary books mentioned in this book in the public libraries, school libraries, college and University libraries. If not there, or if you wish to purchase a book, then look within new and used bookstores. If all fails, or may be in the first instance, go online (computer). You may use the name of the diarist alone or use a book web site. Find a web site by typing out "bookstores" or "book dealers" in a search engine.

In *A Treasury of the World's Great Diaries* (copyright 1957, published by Doubleday and Co., Inc., Gordon City, NY), editors Philip Dunaway and Mel Evans give us, in 586 pages, a few paragraphs of autobiography and some pages from each person's diary (they include eighty-five diarists). I presume they meant that all eighty-five were major diarists. I can't deny them their view and opinion. They list the following (I haven't included those I've already mentioned in my list): Lester Frank Ward, Julia Newberry, John Halliday, John Woolman,

Sarah Kemble Knight, Jacques Marquette, Davy Crockett, Andrew Gordon, Edward Ely, George C. Duffield, Captain Joshua Sears, Edmund Temple, Mark Twain, Queen Victoria, Henri-Frederic Amiel, George Sand, Lord Byron, John Barrymore, Ki No Tsurayuki, Celia Fiennes, Marjory Fleming, The Jesuit Fathers, Thomas Hearne, Thomas Merton, John Wesley, Theodore Upson, Charles E. Davis, Sarah Morgan Dawson, Oliver Wendell Holmes Jr., John Beatty, John Beauchamp Jones, John Milton Hay, Augustus C. Brown, Dolly Sumner Lunt, Lawrence Van Alstyne, Gideon Welles, John Audubon, Edwin Way Teale, Sir Walter Scott, F. Scott Fitzgerald, W.N.P. Barbellion, Selma Lagerlof, Vaslav Nijinsky, Andre Hurault De Maisse, Charles Cavendish Fulke Greville, George Washington, Harold L. Ickes, Pierre Loti, Herman Melville, Louisa May Alcott, Robert Falcon Scott, Lady Kathleen Scott, Jonathan Swift, Samuel Sewall, Thomas Turner, Lady Charlotte Elizabeth Guest, Henry James, Thomas Alva Edison, Arnold Bennett, William Ralph Inge, Philip Hone, Edmond and Jules De Goncourt, Odd Nansen, Harry Levin and Michihiko Hachiya.

Letts published a book entitled *A History of Diary Keeping in Great Britain from 16th-20th Century*. This was for an exhibition that took place on 28 September to 25 October 1987. This book contains pictures of old original diary books, portraits of the many diarists (such as Royalty, Fannie Burney, Victorian Sir Henry Cole, explorer David Livingstone, Harold Nicolson), famous book covers and writing desks (18th century), Queen Victoria's portrait *Sitting Down to Write her diary*, 17th century diarists Evelyn and Pepys, and otherwise covered the great and the minor diarists during the aforementioned time period.

William Matthews compiled *American Diaries – An Annotated Bibliography of American Diaries Written Prior to 1861*. His first diary is that of Rev. Francis Higginson who, in 1629, recorded the days of his voyage from England to New England. Then Matthews lists the 1630 diary of John Winthrop, who was the governor of Boston. The next to last entry is Lester Frank Ward's *An Intimate Diary*. The book contains almost two thousand diarists, including Ralph Waldo

Emerson, Louisa May Alcott and many of the diarists who were Transcendentalists. Other notables are: John Audubon, Adams (John, John Quincy and Abigale), Benedict Arnold, Aaron Burr, John Burroughs, James Ferimore Cooper, Benjamin Franklin, John Fremont and Margaret Fuller.

The same William Matthews then made an annotated list of manuscript diaries; almost all were unpublished. It contains the diaries of over five thousand persons. He lists the names of each diarist, dates of birth and death, and where the manuscripts are located (historical society, University, public library, museum, archive, or other institution). The book is published by the University Press (Georgia), Athens, copyright 1974. For those interested in finding these diaries, this book is invaluable.

Laura Arksey, Nancy Pries and Marcia Reed edited two large volumes (entitled *American Diaries from 1492 to 1980*, copyright 1983). This set goes back one hundred and thirty-seven years before Matthews' *American Diaries*. The list contains Spanish diaries not stated in Matthews' list. These were Spanish explorers in California, New Mexico and the Southwest. Examples are Gaspar de Portola, *California Exploration of 1769 to 1770*, known as "the thousand mile march." Then Father Junipero Serra and the missions of California. The editors believed that even though these diarists were not English colonists and the language was not in English, they wrote them in America and hence should be included. These Spanish diaries have been translated into English.

So to determine whether a diary is of major quality or minor, there are several reference books available. Refer to T*he Treasury of the World's Great Diaries*, look through the lists by Matthews or (refer to the last and most complete set of the Arksey, Pries and Reed, as stated above. The conclusion is yours.

Here is what William Matthews wrote diaries in general and then about Samuel Pepys in his *British Diaries (Covering the Years 1442-1942)*:

"The diarist can see only the pattern of day, not the pattern of a lifetime; if he is a true diarist, one day is likely to be at odds with another for any reader who thinks of people as having fixed characters. People in diaries, like people in real life, are prone to do and to think a variety of odd contrary things that would be regarded as inconsistent and inartistic in the patterned behavior of literature, biography or autobiography. That for me is the real peculiarity and specialness, as well as one of the chief fascinations, of the diary as a way of writing."

Then Matthews wrote of Samuel Pepys:

"Samuel Pepys (1663-1703), Secretary to the Navy Office.

Private diary 1660-1669; the nonpareil of English diaries; the observations and records of a man of infinite variety and zest, "ever with child to see new things"; his own work, domestic life, friendships; and pleasures, which took him into almost every section of English life, from the court to the docks; in its immediacy and variety it is one of the supreme portraits of a man, inside and outside, and a mirror of the times."

Most writers – those who write novels, short stories, columns, books, et al – keep diaries or notebooks. Some of these are just short notes to oneself for their next writing project, while others write more than just notes – they write everything about themselves and what is happening around them. (The latter would be similar to Samuel Pepys and Virginia Woolf.) These latter writers may someday attain the status of a major diarist. Most diaries of the major type take a hundred years to get into those ranks; however, an exception that comes to mind is Anais Nin.

It should not be the intent of the diarist to attain major status. A diary is usually written only for one's self or one's family. If the writing happens to be superior (expressive, observation and content is good) and it also becomes famous, so be it.

One's status in life may or may not be a factor in determining how valuable the diary will be. (Where are you? What do you do? What gifts do you have?) If you are a skipper on a clipper ship and tell the story in great detail, the world will judge whether it's worthy, even though you are not famous. If you are a newspaper reporter and became famous, you keep a more than adequate diary, and your name is Mark Twain, then you have a good chance of being recognized. You teach Mathematics at Oxford and you like to write about little girls, you write *Alice In Wonderland* and *Through the Looking Glass*, and your name is Dodgson (Lewis Carroll). The world will look to your writings as well as into your diary. If you are already famous then we, the world, will want to know more about you; let's read your diary.

Chapter 4

The Diary Process

Observation

When we observe, it's mostly by sight. Of course we observe through the other senses, yet mainly we observe with our eyes. Our eyes tell us what is in the world and what to record. Yet where are we when we observe? Men were sent up in aerial balloons in World War I to observe the enemy. The U.S. Army has a term called "observation post". It originally meant the top of the hill where the enemy was observed in the valley below. Having been in the U.S. Army and in combat, I knew the concept well. Many years later, being a lawyer in Los Angeles, I had my own observation post. I would go to the courthouse cafeteria and take a seat where I could see what was going on in the room. It was a table at the front corner, and while I ate, I could see the lawyers and judges I knew.

One of the nicest places to observe is the garden. There are many living things and activities to record. In my garden I can find the gophers throwing soil into the air but rarely showing themselves. The spy in the garden is the spider, and his web shines in the afternoon sun. The blue spruce has its fingers pointing towards the sky. There is a tall pile of leaves working its way into compost. There are fruit trees which blossom in March – apple, peach, pear, plum and guava. There is a lot more, and I allow my eyes to roam and capture the garden of my neighbor.

How much detail do I put in? Certainly enough to see and make word-pictures.

Then there are combinations of sights, sounds and other senses. A good example is falling rain. The sound it makes depends on how hard it's falling and, at the same time, you can see it. It may also leave a dusky smell.

Henry David Thoreau wrote from the senses of touch, sight, sound and smell. One very early morning before sunrise, he slowly walked into Walden Pond with all of his clothes on, including his shoes. He was careful not to disturb insects or animals. He walked further until the water came up to the point between his mouth and nose. Then he looked for insects, water snails, flowers, new growth on trees, shrubs, the birds and moss around him. He turned his body and looked to the right, then left, then behind.

He did not record what he found right away. He would think, ponder and deliberate all that he saw. He sifted through it and then mixed it with what happened during the remainder of the day. At night before bedtime, he recorded the important aspects of the day in his diary, such as the smell of the forest or the feel of touching the water in the pond or hearing the birds.

<u>Observation Definition</u>

Webster's New Collegiate Dictionary has these words on observation:

1.   act or faculty of observing, or taking notice

2.   an influence drawn from observation or something observed

3.   to pay attention or notice.

Oxford English Dictionary has these words on observation:

1.   the action of observing; the fact observed

2.   the action of an act of paying attention, marking or noticing; the fact of being noticed; notice, remark, perception.

The definition of observation includes all of our senses. It does not rule out acquiring information and facts from other senses: (hearing, smell, touch and taste). I was once in a foxhole with a side room, which was pitch dark. Very soon there was a putrid smell that I could not identify: There was also a dead person in the room. My senses of smell and touch led me to believe a dead person was in there and the decomposing body gave forth the smell. Later I lit a match and used my best sense of sight to gather facts, which corroborated my first findings.

All diarists, young or old, use the power of observation. Opal Whiteley described the trees, woods, animals, people, rivers, a blind girlfriend, and especially her favorite wood rat that lived in her sleeve. It's estimated she did this at age six to eight. Edward Robb Ellis who died in his eighties, wrote and descriptive passages until the very end of his life.

On the subject of observation and feelings, I spoke to Elizabeth Gullander, a spry eighty year old who started her diary at the age of ten. I asked her about observation. She replied, "after you write the observation, then write your feeling about it." I believe she has established the habit of writing her feelings so it comes naturally. Many of us diarists do what she does, especially when the feeling of rage or sorrow sets in, or when extremely happy.

Many diarists have a flair for writing, *joi de vie,* a love for life. Reverend Francis Kilvert seemed to have led the way. Anais Nin had this flair, as well.

Many diarists enjoy recording their impressions of nature. Professor Sarah Rabkin at University of California at Santa Cruz takes students and others on field trips just for that purpose.

In Corralitos, California, under the stately redwoods during late spring, certain types of flies are common. They get in between the tall redwoods where they find sunshine, which energizes them. Then they work like elevators: they fly straight up and then straight down, in a hovering exercise. They travel twenty to fifty feet vertically – up and down, but only in sunshine.

Experimentation

It feels good to experiment in the diary because it's different and unusual. Take the place you call home and write why it is home. I've lived in Corralitos for ten years and have enjoyed it all the way. But I was born in Los Angeles and lived there for 60 years. Corralitos is my retirement home.

So, I think back to my home in Los Angeles. I write and describe the yellow stucco house, the large apricot tree and a lot more. I describe the people who frequented my home. I experiment with the past. I want this information in my diary for my children, my siblings and those that follow me.

You will read later that I write on the right page only. The reason is that the ink may bleed through. I also do this so that the left page may be used for many other purposes. For example, I have sealed (with white glue) flower petals of many colors. The purple, orange, blue and red petals are beautiful and remain with me always.

You might want to use rubber stamps. Saul Steinberg, the artist famous for his drawings in the New Yorker magazine, uses various rubber stamps in his paintings. These are usually stampings showing authority and authenticity. You can do the same.

In Japan, rubber stamps are in fashion. At each castle, house or place of interest, there are rubber stamps showing a picture of a castle, house or place. I've asked the person in charge for permission to use their stamps and have stamped my diary.

When I go to the bank, I've asked clerks at the counter if I could use their rubber stamps. Then I stamp the diary. Later, I write with pencil any words of I want to add.

Here is another story of sight, sound and self-involvement, and also experimentation. John Muir was living alone in Yosemite Valley. There were Indians about but they kept away from him, and yet he knew they were nearby. One sunny day, John Muir of the mountains spotted a grasshopper. Each time he tried to catch it, it jumped and made a peculiar snapping sound. The grasshopper intrigued him. John Muir went after it again and again trying to capture it. He chased this snapping jumper all the way into the Merced River. The snapping stopped and so did the jumping. John grabbed him and closed his hand so he wouldn't get away. Once out of the river, he sat down, took his pocketknife and partially cut both legs so he wouldn't jump and fly again.

John took the grasshopper back to his tent where he got out his diary and stamp pad and pressed the grasshopper's bottom on the stamp pad and commenced to stamp a border on the page. Within the border, he wrote the story of the grasshopper.

Chapter 5

Tools and Supplies

The diarist works with just a few tools, but there are a wide variety of choices in the selection of these tools.

<u>Book</u>

When purchasing, acquiring or making a book, look at all aspects of it. What size is it? Will it fit in my purse or my diary bag? Should it be of shirt pocket size (great when traveling)? The thickness will tell you how long it will take to write and finish it. If it is too thick, it will be difficult to write in, as your wrist must bend to get over the book. There is a rainbow book – the pages are in colors of the rainbow. Do I want to write in such a book? How would I feel writing on red, orange, green and blue paper? Does it say "museum quality paper"? (This means the paper should not yellow in years to come, nor crack.) What are my preferences? – Is the paper lined or unlined? What about the cover? Is there art on the cover or is it plain? Is it a leather, canvas or spiral notebook? These are some of the questions to ask yourself. Virginia and Leonard Woolf owned their own publishing company. They had many types of paper. Virginia would go there, get the paper that suited her, and then would hand make the covers for her diary books by hand.

During the War between the States (1861-1865) and for a period of time thereafter, there were certain types of United States manufactured diary books.

A minister from Indiana traveled to Los Angeles just after the Civil War. Within his diary he recorded the assassination of President Lincoln. Later, he wrote a sad story of his wife's death and the day of her burial, he and his children being in attendance at the gravesite. Upon the minister's demise, his family found twenty-eight Civil War type diaries. In 1975, the 28 volumes were turned over to the bookseller, Jake Zeitlin in Los Angeles. Mr. Zeitlin asked me for a literary valuation and appraisal. These diaries had little monetary value. Since I spent a lot of time reading and evaluating them, the family and Mr. Zeitlin gave me all of the diaries.

From the 28 volumes, I've chosen four to describe. These are from the years 1863, 1871, 1878, and 1902. These are the diaries of the Reverend J. W. Van Clive.

The first book, as stated in the facing page is: *Daily Pocket Remembrances for 1863.* New York (manufacturer) T. G. Shaw & Co. 43 Walker St. It certainly fits into a shirt pocket, at 2 1/2" x 4". The cover is still very strong after 137 years, without a tear. The cover seems to be of some kind of heavy paper or cloth covered with a rosin and then protected with a sealer. There are three spaces per page, one for each day of the year, thus a three-year diary. The space is about 1 1/4", so the writer has 1 1/4" x 2 1/4" to write in per day, therefore the publisher is controlling. If it were my book, I'd feel very controlled. The edges of the paper of the book are tinted in gold color. The last page before the back cover is of a much heavier paper and it accordions out to make a small pocket for stamps or thin paper.

The 1871 book is larger at 3" x 4 3/4". The cover, gold tinting, and the back pocket are the same as the 1863 book. This book gives the writer the entire page to write in (twice as much as the 1863 book).

The book entitled 1878 is printed: "Clergyman's Pocket Diary and Visiting book." It has an index for what a clergyman can use: list of members, funeral of a Christian, records of marriages and so on. There are also several categories for the clergyman to follow, and then the diary pages begin.

The 1902 book is 3" x 5". Same cover, but *red* tinted edges. Its name is the *Excelsior Diary*. There's a lot of printed information before the diary pages begin, such as information about Routes of Travel (to Fresno from San Francisco--fare: $3.75; to Idaho City, Idaho from San Francisco by train--$36.15, by stage--$28.85). Rates didn't change much, as this book was for a year. There was a theater guide of San Francisco, which included opera houses and places of interest. Then there were tables of high water in San Francisco, San Pedro (Los Angeles), Astoria, Oregon, and so on. Also eclipses for 1902, morning and evening stars, and a table of wages. The table of wages showed 5c an hour. A workday was ten hours; ($.05 an hour would be $.50 at the end of the day). Maybe the best chart of all was: 'Things easily Forgotten: Number of watch case _____ ; Number of watch works _____; number of bank book _____; Number of bicycle _____; My weight on _____: _____ lbs.; height _____; Size of my hat (other clothing) _____; This book belongs to _____; In case of accident notify _____, _____, _____."

During World War Two, the Japanese army issued blank diary books to its soldiers. Many of these diary books were found with the deceased soldiers. The American army saw to it that the families of the deceased would receive the soldier's diary. During that same period of time, the United States Army and other combat units would not issue diary books, in fear that they would fall into enemy hands and give away critical information.

Paper

The book, paper (pages) and ink are all one unit. The book's cover and binding are in place to protect the pages. The stronger the binding, cover and boards, the better protected are the pages. I always advise my students to purchase and use a hardback (blank) book. The diary is such a valuable item; the diarist should protect it as best as one can. There are so few pleasures in life, why not spend a little more on a strong book with fine paper.

There are many types of paper. I gave a diary writing class in Los

Angeles in 1976. A young woman wanted to attend, but could not pay the tuition. "Please come; you need not pay" I told her. She attended, and at the end of the class she, being from France, gave me a 1723 oligraph testament – a last will and testament, totally in handwriting (calligraphy) on parchment paper. It was folded in half and then in thirds. I opened it up. The language was in 1723 French. It looked perfect, as if it were written last week. Sheepskin parchment was the paper; it seemed to have an oily quality. I don't believe we can purchase the same paper today. I do know diary books with the words "parchment paper" are being sold, and yet I have examined these sheets of paper and they are manufactured. They are not sheepskin. Maybe the Dead Sea Scrolls were written on sheepskin.

Protection of the Diary Book

Protection from fire: If you have several volumes, bind them with string or by a leather strap, or place them between two bricks. If they're very close together, oxygen cannot get in; without oxygen, there can be no fire. Another safe place is a safe deposit box, *a la* Anais Nin. Or maybe you have or can acquire a fire-proof filing cabinet (a good place, except keep the diary books in the top shelves; there may be a flood, or a washing machine leaking water. If books are in the bottom shelf, water will destroy them just as much as fire).

Writing Instruments

Pen

Do you prefer using a pen, pencil, or the computer? I prefer the pen. My favorite is the fountain pen, not the stick pen or the ballpoint, and not the calligraphy pen. In my desk drawer is a bottle of black ink. The fountain pen is easily filled and writes for a fairly long period of time. The ink runs freely, with little paper drag.

Ballpoint and Felt-tipped Pens

There are ballpoint and felt-tipped pens, some disposable and some with exchangeable inner cores. There are many kinds from the United States and foreign markets. Generally these cost less than $5.00. They write well and come in many colors. You need not use only a fountain pen, as these do well as an adjunct.

Pencil

Originally pencils were encased in wood, and most of them still are. The automatic pencil is encased in metal or plastic; the lead is coaxed out by a twist or push of the instrument.

The question arises as to whether the pencil writing will smear, and if these pencil writings will last any appreciable period of time.

I've proven to myself that pencil writings do not smear. Twenty years ago I wrote several pages in my diary in pencil. I always write with a soft or extra soft lead pencil, #1 or #2. I went back and tested these several pages. The pigment had not changed. It was as dark as it was when first written. I ran my finger over some of the text to intentionally try to smear it; there was no smear.

Reverend Van Clive used a pencil in his diaries over 135 years ago, and there's no sign of smudge or smearing, yet I can't tell if his writing is as dark as when he wrote it.

Inks

For the best of all worlds, it's black ink on white paper. The contrast is greater than other colors. Most black ink does not tend to fade. Other dark color inks I recommend are: dark purple, dark blue, dark deep red, very dark green, very dark brown. Stay away from the light colors of yellow, orange, light red, light green, light brown, and very light blue. You may go back and reread your diary several years later (four to six years or longer) and to find these light inks have faded and are no longer readable. So be careful. There are inks that are supposed to last at least 100 years.

Brush

The famous German author of *The Tin Drum*, Günter Grass, wrote a diary with a paintbrush and brown ink. Not only did he write words, he drew pictures with the same medium. The words in German have been translated into English. The pictures haven't faded. The name of the diary book is "Show Your Tongue." The dustcover contains his pictures, as do the first eight pages. The brush he used seems to have been flat and thin, similar to a calligraphy pen. The strokes are broad to thin.

Diary Bag

The diary bag should be large enough to hold the diary book, another book for reading, space for several pens and pencils, a small stick of glue, and a pair of small scissors.

With this bag you can travel the world and record what comes to you. But you need not travel the world to get the benefit of the diary bag. It's like having a tackle box when going fishing, or a box of tools to make miniature trees (bonsai).

The diary bag should be strong. The best choices are leather and heavy canvas. A shoulder strap is a must for convenience sake.

Take yourself and the diary bag to the beach and have a dialogue with Mother Ocean. Or go to New York City and get to the top steps of the

Metropolitan Museum of Art; then write about all the people going up and down these stairs near you. The diary bag is designed to help you carry your diary so you can write in it when not in your residence.

Chapter 6

Organizing the Diary

Diary writing – which includes general recording, dreams while asleep, jokes, comments, sketches, observations and poetry – will all go systematically within the diary, when organized. This type of book is mainly for hand written diaries, although most of the concepts can be applied to computer diaries.

1. The diary cover (adornment).

It's nice to have a blank book that's interesting and even beautiful to the eye and sensual to the touch. It may also satisfy an artistic temperament. If the book cover is plain with no design or picture, you may do this:

a) Acquire a postcard depicting a master painting and glue it on. It will not only be artistic, it will also tell you the front of the book and which side is up. On my 1999 first volume, I glued a multi-colored postcard to the cover. It's French, with a large man wearing a black hat, a red scarf, and a dark blue over-coat; he's holding a wooden rod. There's a sailor in black silhouette in the background, and on top is the word "Ambassadeurs." It's a handsome card, somewhat large, and it fits the cover well. I enjoy seeing it each time I handle the book.

b) For those who know the art of découpage, the cover is a good place for you to do your art.

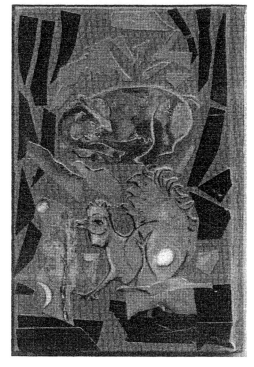

This is the back cover of one of my diary volumes, a découpage from a print by artist Marc Chagall.

2. Inside cover, first page.

In the first writing space, on the inside cover or first page, write your name, address and phone number. This is in case you lose or misplace your diary. The finder will know where to return it.

3. Reward for return of the diary.

After about twenty pages of writing in your diary, the book will become very valuable to you. Simply write near the dedication: "If lost, a reward will be given for its return." My own diaries have been returned to me six times and not one finder would accept a reward.

4. Dedications.

A new diary book is empty without any writing or printing. You may be proud to honor an idea, object or another person. It's important to note here that the dedication may set a tone for the entire book. Here are a few dedications from my past diaries:

a) Volume 55, 11/29/95 – 5/8/96:

I dedicate this volume to my father, Jack Zager. A man I remember always; a kind and shining, jubilant person. He carried me on his shoulders in and out of the Arroyo Seco. He loved to sing and I learned words and melody from him. He was a family man and he and Gertie (my mother) had a large family. I will write this volume with you in mind.

To life – La haiem.

b) Volume 38, 5/12/88 – 8/14/88:

Because this volume will be written mainly in London, Egypt and Israel – I dedicate this volume to those three places.

c) Volume 65, 9/22/99 – 2/23/00:

I dedicate this volume to the men of the 71st Infantry Division and to those of the associates meeting in Cincinnati for the next few days.

5. Date and Place.

When you start writing in the diary, start with the date and place you are writing. Here are a few examples:

a) November 4, 1975. Diamond Jim's restaurant, Sherman Oaks, CA.

b) December 30, 1996. Marriott Hotel, Monterey, CA.

c) September 22, 1992. Emi Restaurant, Santa Cruz, CA.

This information places you in a specific time and place.

6. Numbering of pages.

Number each page on the right side at the bottom. Do not use or number the left page.

7. The left hand page.

The left-hand page is good for:

a) Paste-ons, newspaper or magazine cutouts, postage stamps and other various items.

b) Notes made on separate pieces of paper can be glued in.

c) Flowers can be glued in, or pressed first and then glued in (keep them flat and thin).

8. Last Page.

The last page is the fourth page from the end of the book. (The last three pages are for the index.) It is used as a summary of what took place in the book. Wait until the book is finished to write it. It is best to label the top of the page: "The Last Page." Look for patterns in the diary and what is important to you. (See the attached three copies of "The Last Page", written by me on August 14, 1988, July 26, 1995, and February 23, 2000.)

The Last Page   Aug 14, 1988
Vol 3.8

a record of Egypt, Israel & my cousin
Moshé. then the Barmitzva of Barrett.

Depression lingers.

Books: Diary of Vilna Ghetto, & my diaries,
some how it does not seem to pay to write down all
the books I purchase.

My writing is owing to life: Gunshishin
Layer, Friend g Opal, Tears, My First Car,
Ma's Passover table; I cannot give you my
mother's smile, kisses — the reason that
I joined Holly Prado's creative writing
class.

There is a lot of joy in this diary —
may it stay that way

56

"The Last Page," August 14, 1988.

The Last Page   Vol 54
7-26-1995

I've recorded a great deal in 4 months.
There were weddings, aunt Sophie, Leo, & Sylvia
Pesner died. Lots of pain & lots of joy. Being in
the party for Jeanette 90 b/day was a joy.

So many activities: Dominican Hoop teaching,
decopage - Dad's tackle box, Sophie umbrella purse.
Writing, dreams, hypnogagia, in B'z's class, &
of course this diary.

Doctors & doctors — I've been with them.

Nine entries of depression — she fights me &
I fight her; I can't seem to kill her.

Twice I have been called Liberator, because
of Gunskirken Lager. (Concentration Camp)

Many, in fact all my submission about V E
day were rejected.

My family, immediate are close & loving
to me.

I keep up reading, talking, writing diaries.

Friends write by acting in my life — there
are many.

79

"The Last Page," July 26, 1995.

Last Page 2-23-2000
Vol 65

People in diary & who are important to me: Cousin Bernie
and, Don Monkerman & Carol Hamilton, Alexandra Bray-Valentine,
of Cerise my dear Helen, Patrick & Nancy, maybe Mr. Grigsby, aunt
Jeanette, Elizabeth Lawrence, & JC Watt now deceased; Carol & Russ
Joe Peebles Newmans, Norris Procell, (I did not include family
as by implication they are all included.)

Exciting times: first the reunion of the 71st D in asso
in Cincinnati. Meeting new faces & people.

Then the publishing of Private Zagor
together with readings at Coffee Bean & to the Brothers
Lif members at Temple Bethel.

Creativity: Trip to Washington D.C.
Starting to write book on Diary Techniques.
Bert & Ray — which way is South?
Chief of deaf souls.
Dialogue with age
Moment of the day
Dream running

Down side:
Helen inner ear surgery.
My forehead squeamish surgery.
My eye surgery.
My influenza & pneumonia bout.

Its been a good five months. Toodle do.

"The Last Page," February 23, 2000.

Chapter 7

The Diary Index

An index in a diary points to specific information within the book. Without the index, the diarist will probably hunt for the information for a long time. With the index, all the names, places, ideas, dreams and stories can easily be found.

The three-page Author Inserted Index of September 1999, to February 2000, follows at the end of this chapter, pages 49 to 51. When viewing this index, notice it isn't difficult to find an item in any box. There aren't many entries to a box; ten to seventeen at most.

The top of each box has its own heading; one letter or using three or four letters of the alphabet. The higher producing letters are A, B, C, and D. Z is more heavily used by me, because it's the first letter of my family name. It's obvious the three and four letter boxes contain letters of the alphabet not indexed in the frequency of the one-letter boxes.

Let us physically make up the index. Go to the last three pages of your blank book. Get out a 12-inch ruler. With a pen make a dot at the middle of the page, both vertically and horizontally. This is accomplished by placing the book long side up and then short side up (see Author Inserted Index, page 49). Then draw lines vertically and horizontally, thus making four rectangular boxes. Draw four boxes for each of the three pages.

Look at the Author Inserted Index to see where to place letters A through Z on top of the boxes. The super-structure of the index is now complete. If the instructions are a bit difficult, just look at the samples of the Author Inserted Index on pages 49 to 51.

<u>Names</u>

To help with indexing, most subjects should be given a name. When writing in the diary, it's a good idea to give each subject a name, be it a place, poem, idea, dream, images of sight or sound, and, of course, specific people. This method keeps each subject separate. Then when the name is in the index, it's easy to locate.

One particular person, place or idea may appear several times in the diary. Place the subject as it first appears (in the diary) into the index with the page number after it. Then when it appears again, just place the new page number after the first. Do this with each entry. Please see the Author Inserted Index under B. (Examples: Braz-Valentine and Steve Bankhead).

When starting to index, look at page one of the diary. I assume you have written at least five or more pages. On page one there are persons, things and happenings. You have written things concerning your cousin (whose name is John Adams), about clouds in a dream, and a teacher's meetings. Cousin John Adams' name is placed at the top of Box A, with page number 1 after his name. When John Adams appears on page 10 and 16, it will show as follows:

<u>A</u>

Adams, John 1, 10, 16

"Clouds" and "Dream" are to be cross-referenced under C & D.

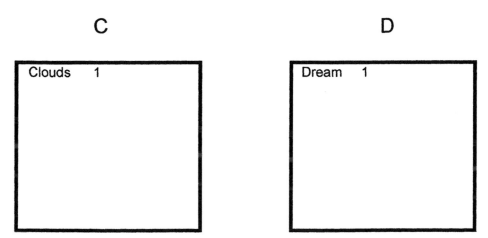

Teacher meeting would go with T (in the S.T.U.V. Box). Cross-referencing Teacher Meeting is within the determination of the diarist.

In a blank diary book of 200 pages, just 100 should be written upon, excluding the three-page index, and the Last Page. Remember that the left side is not written on. Assuming the diary book is a regular size of 7 1/4" x 8 3/4", the number of entries per index box will be less than fifteen. Look at the Author Inserted Index: all boxes have fifteen entries or less, with the exception of K.L.M. and S.T.U.V. All entries are placed into an alphabetical box, with easy access by the diarist. It's not difficult to run a finger down one of the boxes to find your entry.

The plus sign, (+): The plus sign indicates the left side of the page. You may place a stamp, picture, short newspaper article, or other item on the left side of the page. When you want to find these items, when indexing, use the stamp name – it could be Pacific Coast Rain Forest, a picture of your brother, a Mercury News article on Samuel Pepys, etc.. After each of the entries, place the number of the right side page and include the plus sign.

K.L.M.

Mercury News 26+

N.O.P.

Pepys, Samuel 26+

Start indexing when you have completed 20 pages or less. If you wait until there are many more pages to index, then the task of indexing may become a burden. It must be stated here that indexing your own diary can be fun and rewarding. You get to reread your diary when indexing. All the people's names, places, your use of words, special sayings, and many other ideas will come up. You have written for, say, several weeks, and many little items have been lost to your present memory. Ideas and items have slipped away. Then you think, "Oh, I'm glad I recorded what I did". Personally, the information is very valuable to me. If I did not record it, it would be lost forever. Look at the Author Inserted Index, Box A: I read a book on Andersonville Prison, Messrs. Alcala and Frusetta phoned and congratulated me on my book *Private Zager*, another new book is waiting to be written on John and Abigail Adams. Just these few items are valuable to me. It takes me back to when these matters happened, which is a good feeling.

The index is a shorthand version of the text in the diary. Many times the index will satisfy the inquiry without going to the text. In the Author Inserted Index under E.F.G., there is the name Gullander, Elizabeth. She made such an impression on me. She's 81, and she has been writing a journal since age ten. Just her name tells me what I want to know, as we had just two meetings together. Another example under K.L.M. is the name Library of Congress and

Copyright Office 21. I need not read page 21, as I remember in detail how I took my published book, filled out a form, paid a fee, and had it registered. One reason why I remember it so well is that almost every author mails his or her published work in. What's important is that it is there in the index and the text.

A subject with several numbers after it represents several pages in the text. In the Author Inserted Index, find Braz-Valentine, Claire and Bankhead, Steve. There are seven numbers after the Braz-Valentine name, and three after the Bankhead name. I cannot remember the background of each added number. In this situation you would turn to the text to get the information needed. So you can remember each situation represented by a number, use a hook. See the name Angel, Bernie, in the Author Inserted Index, where I placed the word "accident" as a hook. This word hooks my memory to the conversation that I had with him and his terrible accident. Another hook is in Box B – "Book about Diaries" 4 (Writer's Digest). The hook is "Writer's Digest," a conversation with friends who stated that this book would be a good choice for this publisher. Another example is Day, Moment of (sunroof down) 59. The key, or hook is "sunroof down." Without this key, the language would point me in a hundred directions and I would have to go to the text. With the key, my memory is reawakened and the key alone tells me Helen and I stopped next to a park in Capitola just to rest or meditate. The back portions of the front seats in the Maxima were put down, and the sunroof opened. Being on our backs we could see out of the sunroof, up the trees close to us, the open sky, clouds and birds in the trees. So put in the hooks, the keys. Just one word or two, and it will save you a lot of time.

Author Inserted Index of September 1999, to February 2000. (Pages 49-51)

A

A novel physical 35
Undignable prices 36
A koala, a Fluxette 43
A leporcha & body found 51
Angel, Bernie - accident 52
Adams, John & Abigail 67, 68
alvin cousin 73

B

Bacon, Harry 2, 6 (anne) Haymut 7.
Book club Marion 4 (u intend digest),
Being alive twice 5 +
Blackwell, M.D - Eye surgery 12, 66
Broz Valentine 15, 18, 41, 49, 55, 58, 63
Bankhead, Steve 26, 30, 56
Brendal, Carol 41, 50
Brotherhood, Synagogue 43 Michaelman,
Bookshops/erry - Ingrid 44 Xeloy,
Bert & Ray: which way 4 south? 47, 52
Barkley 50
Being alone - pleasures, doing 52
Bothner, Patricks Nancy Shino 60
Boston public Library 67

C

City tour 8
Colored pens 14
Chelsea Flower Show 18
Copycenter Coffee Bean 26, 30, 31
Capitola ok cafe 28, 29
Cardona, Karen 43
Command, coke 56
Cardiology office 58,
Cogaler, Yitz Reb 64, 66, 69, 70
Chief of Dead Souls - but
are they 73, not live 74

D

Depression 22, 23 q me, 45
dialogue - did not dur but 25
Diary Technique (book) 37, 66
Disaster, yesterday wee 45
Duplicate book list for sale 51
Dialogue with age 52 Bert & Ry 47
Dietz, jogle 55
Decisive moment 57
Day, moment of (sun roof dn) 59
Dream - running 63
Diary exhibit 69
Deadbook, chig 73

A-D Index.

E-P Index.

Q-Z Index.

Chapter 8

Dialogues

Does the writing of dialogues belong in a diary?

A diary is to make a record of your life that you may want to keep. (If you want it to be preserved, it's best to keep a strong hardback book for this purpose.) If you write a dialogue that you also want to keep as part of your work (as a writing that may or may not be published at a later time), then the answer is yes – dialogues belong in a diary.

Webster defines dialogue as, "A written composition representing two or more persons as conversing or reasoning; the conversational element, as in literary or dramatic composition."

Dialogues can be between two or more persons or between a person and an object. A substantial part of Dr. Ira Progoff's book *At a Journal Workshop* relates to the dialogues between a person and an object.

I've written many dialogues between a person and an object. These dialogues are in my diary because the diary book is with me most of the time (and it's the best place for me to write).

So how does a person get started writing a dialogue?

It's simple, really. You say to yourself, "I want to write or talk to another person or object." To see how it goes let's dialogue with an object on your desk; for example, a ball point pen. You can ask the question, "Why are you here?" The object speaks first.

<u>Pen</u>
Because you bought me and placed me here.

Me

I mean more than that. How were you made?

(The pen takes on the personality of a young Japanese woman.)

Pen

I was put together in Japan.

Me

What's your name?

Pen

Just read my imprint – "Pentel – Rolling Writer –

Japan."

Me

Were you made or constructed in a factory?

Pen

Oh, yes! In a factory.

Me

What materials did they use?

Pen

I'm afraid to tell.

Me

Why?

Pen

Well, a girl does not like to talk about her innards and

her make up.

Me

No one will overhear us.

Pen

Well, alright.

Me

Let's talk about what you're made of.

<u>Pen</u>

Well, I'm mostly plastic with an ink cartridge. Oh yes,

I have a metal clip.

<u>Me</u>

You left out two items.

<u>Pen</u>

I know my color; purple on my barrel represents the

color of the ink and the engraving on the metal clip

states my name.

_____

Dr. Progoff believes that before you dialogue, it would be a good idea to be still, with your eyes closed for 10 minutes. My best dialogues have come from imagery of hypnogogia, night dreams and meditations. Please refer to those chapters.

When you dialogue with another person or an object, a particular situation comes into play. When you write for yourself, you know exactly what you're saying or writing; but that's not true with the other person or object. Because you don't know what the other person or object will say, you're surprised by the content of the statement. This unknown is always an amazement, making dialogue writing unusual and a joy to do. In my dialogue, the pen not only took on a personality; her statements were from a different place. I believe that the pen's statements come from my imagination or my unconscious.

<u>Hypnopompic</u>

You're coming out of sleep. Your mind is very clear. You have been in one place, in sleep for several hours, with no telephone ringing, no radio or television, no talking. You are calm and serene. In this state, your mind is fresh and can connect and concentrate. Let's assume you've had an argument with your best friend. It's on your mind, at awakening. You put on a robe and slippers and go to your writing table.

You begin –

Best Friend

Why do you treat me so harshly and like dirt?

Me

I don't intend to.

Best Friend

But you do it any way.

Me

I'll try and remember not to insult you.

Best Friend

If you try we can be even better friends.

Me

I'm glad I talked to you.

A dialogue between an object or a fictitious person

A dialogue entitled "A Little Figure Appeared and Talked to Me" came to me, in a hypnopompic state, after I visited a scientist in his laboratory in the city of Boston. The scientist had invented a machine, which would keep track of aircraft circling an airport, and was also used to study earthquakes.

The machine looked like a large stainless steel chair (about ten times larger than a dining-room chair). It was made of high-tempered steel, with a large electric motor attached. Tied to the chair by steel springs was a highly polished steel mirror. When the machine was turned on, the mirror would vibrate at thousands of times per minute. The mirror and other factors of the machine threw an image into the room. The image was a silver color almost the size of a dinner plate. The machine could move it about the room. It was in mid-air and not touching or attached to anything. I was told I could touch it or hit it with my hand. I hit it and went right through it. Nothing happened, it was just there. It was nothing more than an image in the space of the room.

About six months after witnessing the image in space, I came out of a hypnopompic state, and wrote this dialogue.

A Little Figure Appeared and Talked to Me

Figure
Hi there!

Me
Who are you and why are you here?

Figure
I'm just me and I popped into existence.

Me
What do you mean, "popped?"

Figure
Well, a few moments ago I was nothing and now I am
someone.

Me
Were you born?

Figure
I suppose.

Me
Do you have a mother?

Figure
No.

Me

You don't have a mother? Did you come from a seed

or an egg?

Figure

No, no. It just happened.

Me

Doesn't make sense.

Figure

I am here to give you a gift.

Me

Yeah, what kind?

Figure

Well, what is your most enjoyable activity?

Me

Enjoyment for me is a pinball machine, or live plants,

or cats.

Figure

Well, your first answer is probably what you want.

Me

Yeah, a pinball machine.

Figure

Do you have one in mind?

Me

You bet. The latest model – electronic.

Figure

I was thinking one not so expensive.

Me

Well, that's what I want. Pinball machines started in

the early 1920's and have matured over the years.

Who are you?

Figure

I'm an image in space.

Me

What!?

Figure

Look at me.

Me

OK – I am. This whole thing is grabbing my rump.

Figure

Notice that I am not attached to anything.

Me

So?

Figure

I am a being with no substance.

Me

OK.

Figure

You can see me and hear me, but I am only an image

in the air.

Me

Let's see if you can withstand a left hook.

Figure

Yes, please try. See – you went through me as if I

were not here.

Me

Do you know why you exist?

Figure

Yes, to present you with a gift.

Me

That's your sole reason to exist?

Figure

I believe that's true.

Me

What happens after the gift's made?

Figure

Then, poof! I'm out of existence.

Me

Who put you up to this?

Figure

I promised I'd never tell.

Me

Is it a man, woman or a machine?

Figure

Peeka boo – I see you and drop dead like lead.

Me

Hey, wait a minute. I answered your question and now you should answer mine.

Figure

Listen to me, buster – I can go poof and be gone and you will not get your pinball machine.

Me

To heck with the pinball machine. I'd rather have you.

Figure

Oh, so you think I am property for you to do with as you wish?

Me

Well, aren't you?

Figure

Well, I'm not a storekeeper, not land, not cash, not a freckle and not running water.

Me

Well, what are you?

Figure

As I said, I am an image and not in color, either. My
natural color is silver.

Me

An image in the color silver.

Figure

That's right buster and you can smoke it!

Me

Well, the best thing for me is to take the pinball
machine and say goodbye.

Figure

Don't you want to know why you're getting this gift?

Me

Yes. I suppose so.

Figure

Because you are a good person.

Me

That's it; I can't stand you. I don't want the pinball
machine.

Figure

Did I offend you by saying you are a good person?

Me

No – but I just don't believe you. Where did you get
these facts that say I'm such a good person?

Figure

Why, it's written all over you're face.

Me

Take a hike, figure.

Figure

Do you want me to go?

Me

That's the message.

Figure

Here it is and it's a lovely gift, too.

Me

Something for nothing. After I've kicked the gift horse

in the mouth.

Figure

Well, my work is done and I must leave.

Me

Where will you go?

Figure

Back to the hospital computer.

Me

What? Say that again.

Figure

Back to the hospital computer.

Me

Which hospital?

Figure

Go play with your brand new electronic pinball

machine. Go ahead and plug it in.

Me

Why a hospital computer?

Figure

I plugged in the pinball machine. Do you have a

quarter?

Me

Sure.

Figure

Well, put it in the machine and push the button that says, "Start."

Me

Will you watch?

Figure

Si, Senior.

Me

Who put you together?

Figure

Why not start the game?

Me

Do I belong in the hospital?

Figure

Only your doctor knows.

Me

Have you been to the hospital?

Figure

Remember, I was born there.

Me

Have you seen me at the hospital?

Figure

Yes.

Me

Am I due back? Did I escape?

Figure

The pinball machine is yours for coming back.

Me

I thought a gift was not in payment.

Figure

What difference does it make? It will make the

hospital stay that much easier.

Me

You're not my friend. Your allegiance is to the

hospital computer.

Figure

Hey, man; this is the electronic age.

Me

How did you find me?

Figure

You left clues even a baby could recognize.

Me

You won't force me?

Figure

Not me, the authorities.

Me

Is your pinball machine an illusion?

Figure

You betcha my silver it is!

Me

This whole chatter is a farce.

Figure

Won't you come quietly?

Me

Do I have an even chance?

Figure

No, man – the cards are stacked against you.

Me

How many cards?

<u>Figure</u>

The building is filled with police and hospital male
nurses.

_____

Power of the Dialogue

If you have a habit you want to break, dialogue with the habit. I'd been coughing a lot from my cigarette habit. I'd been trying to quit. Why not face the cigarette habit with a dialogue?

<u>Smoking Habit</u>

Well, I've gotcha again!

<u>Me</u>

Damn you! It's been all your way lately.

<u>Smoking Habit</u>

Ha! Ha! Ha! – And you think you could stay away

from me?

<u>Me</u>

Well, I've tried and Helen is on my side – she saw an

article on lung cancer and we talked about it.

<u>Smoking Habit</u>

You're not worth a straw in a dung heap.

<u>Me</u>

What do you mean?

<u>Smoking Habit</u>

You have no guts and when I'm through with you –

you'll die an early age because I'll kill you!

<u>Me</u>

Why, you should be outlawed. I feel like a good fight

and I'll take you on. I'll put you out of my life forever.

All you have to fight with is my persistent feeling and

desire for nicotine.

<u>Smoking Habit</u>

But that's enough, eh?

<u>Me</u>

No it's not! I've taken my pocketknife out of my pocket

and it's been sharpened to a razor's edge. I've just

cut your throat and you are bleeding – bleeding all

over me; over my hands, my pants and my shoes.

Now you're dead. You're gone, Halleluya!

All the above was recorded in my diary on January 16, 1980. Whenever I see a cigarette, I see blood. I never smoked again after that date.

<u>Go back to Your Childhood</u>

I remembered my mother saying to me when I was eight, "Ray, it's not right or good for you to look into your grandparents chest of drawers." When she said that I felt guilty, yet I wanted to get back to that time period. I decided to dialogue with my grandmother's mirror.

<u>My Grandmother's mirror</u>

Ray, What do you see?

Look, it's alright, no one else is here – they won't

mind – look into Ma and Pa's dresser drawer.

<u>Me</u>

You're an old mirror aren't you?

<u>My Grandmother's mirror</u>

Yes.

Me

Did you come from Russia?

My Grandmother's mirror

No, just a secondhand store on N. Figueroa Street.

Me

If I look in the dresser – will you tell them?

My Grandmother's mirror

They don't talk to me.

Me

Ok – Let's you and I look.

My Grandmother's mirror

Now you're talking.

Me

Oh! Pa's underwear – and Ma's stockings – Oh! –
here are the coat buttons made from gold Russian
coins.

My Grandmother's mirror

Be sure and put them back the way you found them
or all will know you were in there.

Me

Oh! Oh! I don't remember.

My Grandmother's mirror

How old are you?

Me

Eight.

My Grandmother's mirror

Did you intend to steal anything?

Me

I don't think so – I'm just curious.

My Grandmother's mirror

I wouldn't tell anyway – no one would believe me.

Me

Are you friends with the mirror in the bathroom?

My Grandmother's mirror

We don't speak at all – the mirror sees all the toilet

problems and that makes me sick.

Me

My grandma is very pretty, isn't she?

My Grandmother's mirror

Oh – yes!

Me

Do you like her perfume and rouge – I do.

My Grandmother's mirror

Yes – and a lovely old world charming lady and face

to put it on as well.

Me

Well – Ma is about to come in from the garden – so I'll

go into the living room – Bye!

My Grandmother's mirror

Here's looking at you! – Bye!

————————

Dialogue with a Wisdom Figure

We all have or maybe would like to have a wisdom figure of our own. A wisdom figure is some person living or dead, or an object, in which you have a good and close feeling. A person or object in which you can converse with or solve problems, get to your feelings and try to get answers.

How can you find a wisdom figure? The way I was taught is that the wisdom figure will come to me once I give an opening.

Open yourself up. A person must first choose at least twelve persons and/or objects, as one of these will be your wisdom figure.

To be sure, make a list of twenty or more, and then pair them down to twelve.

The list of wisdom figures may be one or more of the following persons (these are examples only, you make up your own list): Benjamin Franklin, Madam Curie, George Washington, Virginia Woolf, Abraham Lincoln, Famous Fannie Burney, John Muir, Rosa Parks, Ralph Waldo Emerson, Eleanor Roosevelt, Henry David Thoreau, Nell Gwyn, Gen. George Patton, Anais Nin, Andre Gide, Margaret Fuller, Teddy Roosevelt, Opal Whiteley, Franklin Delano Roosevelt, Louisa May Alcott, Oliver Wendell Holmes, Sr. (poet), Abgiail Adams, Oliver Wendell Holmes, Jr. (Chief Justice to the Supreme Court), Anne Frank, Napoleon Bonapart, Katherine Mansfield, William Wordsworth, Selma Lagerlof, Samuel Coolerage, Marjorie Fleming, George Washington Carver, George Sand, Martin Luther King, Jr., and Queen Victoria.

List of objects: Rosetta Stone, Statue of Liberty, Statue of Robert E Lee (in New Orleans), Magna Carta, U.S. Constitution, The Bill of Rights, The Liberty Bell, Eiffel Tower, Golden Gate Bridge, U.S.S. Constitution (also known as "Old Iron Sides"), Library of Congress, Pacific Ocean, Mt. Everest, Death Valley, Jack Benny's car (the Maxwell), U.S.S. Macon (Navy Dirgible), and the Mississippi River.

Make your own list from the names and objects above, but mainly from your own sources. If you have more than twenty, eliminate to twelve, i.e., those less likely to be chosen. Remember – you will eventually get down to one.

Now to eliminate eleven of the twelve remaining. Picture yourself in a large auditorium looking at a lighted stage. Take your twelve choices and have them stand across the stage with space between them so you can see each one quite clearly. Have them take up most of the width of the stage.

Now look at all twelve on the stage. Do not pick one. Instead, wait a little while; one of the characters or objects will pick you out by walking to the front of the line. This person or object is your wisdom figure.

It's now time to dialogue with your wisdom figure.

The first question you want to work on is: How did you acquire your ethics? Ask him, her, or the object that question. Let's assume Virginia Woolf picked you out. Start like this:

Me

Virginia, where did I acquire my ethics?

Virginia Woolf

My dear one, it was probably your parents. Did they
have good parents, did they go to church?

Me

I'm a foster child, my parents died when I was quite
young.

Virginia Woolf

Were you close to your foster parents?

Me

We were quite close, a loving relationship and with
foster siblings as well.

Virginia Woolf

How about your grandparents?

Me

I never knew them.

<u>Virginia Woolf</u>

Who were your role models?

<u>Me</u>

My Aunt Lillian.

<u>Virginia Woolf</u>

Did you spend time with her as a young person?

<u>Me</u>

Oh, yes, lots of time.

<u>Virginia Woolf</u>

Did she teach you right from wrong?

<u>Me</u>

I don't remember any specific times, but in my mind I
see her always doing the right thing.

———————————

This is how it works. You can ask any question of your wisdom figure.
Try it, and practice, and it will come in handy when you need it.

<u>Here's an example of a dialogue with an object (the Liberty Bell)</u>

<u>Me</u>

I've heard about you but really don't know you.

<u>Liberty Bell</u>

Well, I'm tough, strong and make a loud piercing
sound when hit.

<u>Me</u>

Can I ask you a question?

<u>Liberty Bell</u>

I'm here to help.

<u>Me</u>

Do you think I can help my country?

<u>Liberty Bell</u>

What kind of help does your country need?

<u>Me</u>

The people, persons who run the country need help.

<u>Liberty Bell</u>

What do they need?

<u>Me</u>

Guidance.

<u>Liberty Bell</u>

In what way?

<u>Me</u>

When making judgements.

<u>Liberty Bell</u>

I'll buy that. Sure, help them all you can – letters,

telegrams, voice mail – go to it.

Ideas of whom to dialogue with and why

Illness

Let's assume you're ailing from the flu and you want to get to know why you're ill. Dialogue with your body. Talk to your body. You will probably get answers like this: "You have not treated me right. You played too hard, too swiftly, caught a chill, and furthermore you're not eating the good foods – all that fast, non-nutritious food. You also read too late at night and are not getting enough sleep."

Dreams

Dreams come at night while a person is asleep and during the day, in daydreams. Similar to dreams, although not literally dreams, are hypnogogic and hypnopompic images. When one of these dreams or images come to you, you may want to know more about them.

You may want to dialogue with the dream; but first give the dream a name. Ask the dream questions and allow it to answer. You can also dialogue with part of the dream, or a person or object in the dream.

Example: the name of my dream is – "Driving up a Hill." In the dream, my family and I are in our car. We're driving up a long and steep hill. We get three-quarters up the hill, but then our car slides backwards to the bottom. We try again, this time we get half way up and then slide to the bottom again. This happens four separate times.

The dream is quite puzzling to me and I cannot make it out, can't understand it.

I could dialogue with the persons in the car (my wife or my small children) or the car. Probably best to dialogue with my car. The car speaks first.

Car

I don't really know why I couldn't make it up and over
the hill. Heck! You were the driver.

Me

The road was blacktopped with no ice, snow or
gravel.

Car

I seem to have plenty of gas and a recent tune up.

Me

Maybe your engine and transmission system is just
not strong enough.

Car

Now wait a minute buster! – I'm damn strong and
tough. I'm made of metal, plastic and glass put
together by world class mechanics.

Me

Dreams are not black and white. Maybe it's a
metaphor for something else.

Car

That's it, I'm just a metaphor, look elsewhere to solve
your problem.

Me

Let's see – I go up the hill and then I slide back; it's
my dream so it has to be something about me.

Car

Remember I'm your metaphor; look into your
bedroom mirror.

Me

OK, mirror, what is it? Oh, I believe I've solved the
puzzle. It's my finances. I get ahead, earn and save
money, and then there's a dry period when my bank
account runs out. Then I must work long and hard to
rebuild my bank account, and then it happens again
and again. My conscience is saying – do something
about this; it's a major problem. Sliding back literally
is the same as the money sliding out of my account.

Animals

When animals talk, or use body actions, to point out a moral at the end of
a story, it's called a fable.

All animals can talk if you give them the voice. I've written fables with a large brown snail, a mouse (the larder) and a yellow jacket. (Hey lady, my jacket is yellow; look at it, I'm not a bee.)

The fable (story) usually happens while you're writing but with the animal in mind. My dialogue story of Mr. Brown Snail happened when I walked in my back yard and saw him on a large leaf. I went to my desk and dialogued with him. This is how it went:

A Mollusk known as "Mr. Brown Snail"

Walking into Helen's studio, I saw a large brown snail eating away at a large green leaf of the datura tree. I grab him. He speaks.

Mr. Brown Snail

What are you doing?

Me

Well, I was about to put you on the ground and step
on and crush you.

Mr. Brown Snail

Why you half-cocked dirty volcano! This is my life
you're playing with. How dare you. You terrible oaf. I
demand that you leave me alone. What gives you the
right to interfere with my life?

Me

Okay, okay, okay. You are quite talkative – where did
you learn to talk?

Mr. Brown Snail

I can ask you the same: where did you learn to talk?
Ha, ha, where did you learn to talk?

Me

Do you claim to be of the same status as a human being?

Mr. Brown Snail

I'm not of the same status – just a different status, with rights, hopes and hunger. So stay away from me tyrant! Hitler! Killer! Can't you stay in your world and leave us mollusks alone?

Me

What do you really want, Mr. Snail?

Mr. Brown Snail

What do I really want? I want a homeland, like Israel is for the Jews. A place where my species will not be molested and killed by humans and others. A place where there are plenty of trees, shrubs and plants. Mr. Whoever-you-are, have you noticed that when a mollusk eats a leaf, that he or she never eats it all – never kills the plant? Have ya'? Have ya'? Have ya'? Probably you're so stupid that you never recognized the situation.

Me

But Mr. Brown Snail, if you eat a hole in our datura tree leaf, it destroys the beauty of it.

Mr. Brown Snail

Beauty, snooty – and to whom? We mollusks take the opposite position; we believe we make perfect types of holes, which make for more beauty.

Oh! Oh! Here comes the killer!

Helen walks up.

Helen

What's going on, dear?

Mr. Brown Snail goes into his shell for protection.

Me

Honey, I was talking to Mr. Brown Snail, who

complains that he has a right to live and eat and that

you are a killer of mollusks.

Mr. Brown Snail

I must say my piece. This woman you call "Honey" is

noted by the mollusk kingdom as the worst killer of

snails in the Fairfax district. She gets a special thrill

when she finds one of us and puts us on the ground

and steps on us. If I had the means, I would do the

same to her.

Helen

Ray, don't just stand there, kill that miserable pest;

snails like him ruin my garden.

Me

How do you like that? – I'm caught between a wife

and a brown snail.

Mr. Brown Snail

It's time you got rid of her, Ray; we don't have the

tools or means, but you do. The entire flock, family

and groups of snails would make you our Moses.

Ray

Hey, I have an idea for you both to hear. Helen and

Mr. Brown Snail listen: we have a corner of the

garden with two trees and other foliage. If we (Helen

and I) gave you this part of the garden, would you

leave the rest alone?

Helen

I'm not sure, I will have to think about it – you know,
sleep on it.

Mr. Brown Snail

I can only speak for myself, but I'll speak to the rest of
them and come back tomorrow with an answer.

In the morning at breakfast, Helen and I have a chat.

Helen

Ray, I didn't like the way you handled matters
yesterday – you really took Mr. Brown Snail's side. I
don't want any snails in any part of the yard. I hate
snails; they're disgusting. They destroy flowers,
leaves, plants. No, I have made up my mind – I'll kill
any, all, and especially Mr. Brown Snail in my yard.
Do you hear that? There is no appeasement here.

Ray

What will happen when Mr. Brown Snail appears with
his report? Will you kill him on the spot or will you kill
him after his report; or later or not at all?

Helen

When he appears, I'll grab him, throw him against the
wall (that'll crack his shell), and then I'll step on him
and grind him into the dirt and there will be no more
Mr. Brown Snail.

Ray

Hey, now, wait a minute. You made an agreement to
wait till today and listen to his side and I believe you
ought to do that; hear him out. Then if you're not
satisfied with his answer – well, I'll take him to another
part of the city. At least we will live up to the bargain.

Helen

No! No! No! I hate that Mr. Brown Snail and off
comes his shell and I'll squish his body. I know I am
mad when it comes to snails – so I'll let you run the
show.

In the afternoon, Mr. Brown Snail appears with a light blue shelled mollusk (snail)
who speaks out.

Light Blue Snail

Hear yea! Hear yea! Hear yea! Mr. Brown Snail, a
mollusk, is empowered by Beverly-Fairfax clan of
snails to place before the residence of Helen and Ray
Zager the following proclamation.

Mr. Brown Snail appears on a large green datura leaf with many papers in his
mouth.

Mr. Brown Snail

Helen and Ray and all mollusks within the call of my
voice: last night meetings were held between the
streets of Melrose, La Cienega, Beverly and Fairfax.
The question put before two million, six hundred and
forty thousand, and two hundred and eleven snails
was whether a snail would restrict or confine his rights
to eat and lodge to a part of the garden when the
whole garden exists. The issue contained the
agreement that the snails would not be hurt, killed or
manipulated in any way. And the total vote is: by
each and every of the two million, six hundred and
forty thousand, and two hundred and eleven mollusks
– No! Absolutely not. The main reason being that
you, Ray and Helen, and every other human being do

not own, control, nor are you entitled to the entire
garden.

Let me also say this to Helen. If you try in any way to
injure me now, let me just tell you that there are two
million, six hundred and forty thousand, and two
hundred and eleven mollusks on your property right
now. Look around Helen – we are on every leaf in
your garden. In minutes, most or all of the vegetation
would be gone. Our only choice, Helen is to tolerate
each other and live with each other!

<u>Helen</u>

That's what you think, you-you-you… brown, ugly,
gastropod mollusk!

Helen grabs Mr. Brown Snail and is about to kill him, when many small voices
rang out.

<u>Many Snail Voices</u>

Helen, we are about to make our first chomp.

I grab Helen's arm and snatch Mr. Brown snail, uninjured. I shout to all of the
two million, six hundred and forty thousand, and two hundred and eleven
mollusks.

<u>Ray</u>

I am donating the south side of the house to you and
if you come into any other area, you are on your own
– the risk is yours.

<u>Many Snail Voices</u>

It's no deal!

I take Mr. Brown Snail into the house, after taking a datura tree leaf. I put Mr. Brown Snail on the leaf and place it on a side table near my favorite lounging chair.

Ray

You know, Mr. Brown Snail, we are like Northern
Ireland, like Arabs and Jews; do you believe there will
be peace between us?

Mr. Brown Snail

It may take centuries. I believe some day it will
happen. I like your cozy home – especially the
fireplace.

Ray

Mr. Brown Snail, do you like me; can we be friends?

Mr. Brown Snail

Ray, we do get along, you understand we mollusks
and our rights. Are there more people on this earth
like you?

Conclusion: As you can see, the dialogue can be used in many situations (and many places not mentioned). I've dialogued with Mother Ocean while sitting at her shore. My best and most satisfying dialogues have been with my deceased friend, Bert. Bert is special, he says what he wants, and uses his hard language. I suggest that you can use the dialogue techniques in this and also the following chapters: Meditation, Dreams, Hypnogogic Imagery and Hypnopompic Imagery. In conclusion, dialogues can be a vital part of your writing.

Chapter 9

Meditation

To write after a meditation is wonderful. You're in a state of calmness and, perhaps, serenity. You've stilled the mind. Writing under and within this state is where many writers want to be. Why is this so?

For one reason, the mind is clear and in a relaxed state. The body is rested, and ready and willing to go to work, or to play. You'll understand, when it happens to you.

The State of Meditation

There are many ways to get into the state of meditation (*alpha* or *alpha-theta* brainwaves). It's like traveling: you can walk, cycle, take a bus, train or plane. Some techniques of meditation suggest concentrating on an object; others use a mantra (words and/or sounds that are repeated), while other techniques involve focusing on the air going in and out of the nose-mouth, as well as counting your breaths. (See Le Shan's *The Art of Meditation*, and also Daniel Goleman's, *The Meditative Mind*.)

After meditating for twenty minutes, you may be able to go from beta brainwaves to alpha brainwaves. The alpha state is one of four major brainwave frequencies. The one that occurs during the day is beta, at 30-13 cycles per second (normal wakefulness); the next one, alpha, is slower at 12-8 cycles per second (passive alertness, light meditation); theta is still slower at 7-4 cycles per second (deep meditation, believed to be related to creative mental activity); and delta is the slowest of all, at 3-1 cycle per second (deep non-rem sleep).

In the book, *Hypnagogia*, author Andreas Mavromatis discusses the eight stages of meditation of Patanjali's Yoga Sutras (as does Daniel Goleman in his book, *The Meditative Mind*). The first four stages deal with the <u>reduction</u> of psychophysical disturbances (two of these have to do with quieting the emotions and desire, and the other two relate to the reduction or elimination of noise). The next stage involves psychophysical withdrawal and the stage following that has to do with limiting the attention and concentrating on an object or image for a period of time. The last stage further continues the maintenance of attention, which is said to be "absorbed" in the object, and the dissolution of the subject.

<u>Counting your Breaths</u>

The method I've used for over twenty-five years is called, "concentrating on counting one's breaths." It's a method that takes about twenty minutes and it's quite easy to learn.

First, it's best to put your body in a comfortable position. So you'll be in a relaxed state. Use a comfortable chair, recliner or your bed. I find that the more comfortable and relaxed you are to begin with, the better the outcome. On a recliner or bed, I find that lying on your back is best. Lying on one's side does not work as well.

<u>Quiet the mind as well.</u> Close your eyes, and cover them in the daytime. I have a hallway with no windows, and when the only two doors are closed, it's in darkness. (This is a very good place to meditate during the day.) If you're meditating when there's light outside, it's best to cover the eyes so no light comes through the eyelids (a mask or a dark cloth will do). If you're meditating at night, it's best in the dark without any lights on.

Once you're in a very comfortable position, in a darkened room, with your eyes closed and your body and mind relaxed, then start counting your breaths. Take a breath and let it out. Count only the out-going breaths. Practice that a little while, until you understand how it works.

Then count each breath until you reach the number twenty-six and repeat this ten times. Twenty-six numbers are used, because that's the same amount of numbers as there are letters in the alphabet; sometimes you may want to use letters.

While you're comfortable, and counting out-going breaths, other ideas, pictures and extraneous matters will come into your mind. This can't be avoided. When they come in, recognize them, delete them, then go on concentrating on the breaths and counting them. After twenty-five years since I've used this system, these extraneous matters still come in. I just go back to my concentration and give them no worth; don't think or worry about these thoughts.

How much time? The usual length of time to meditate is twenty minutes to half an hour. You can look at the clock or a watch to determine the amount of time left, or use a system to measure time. I use what I call "crooking the fingers system." My hands are open when sitting, or reclining, or lying on the bed. Counting my out-breaths from one to twenty-six takes two minutes. When I reach twenty-six, I crook my little finger back to the palm of my hand and hold it there. I continue with the counting until I reach twenty-six again. Then I crook the ring finger to the palm and hold it there. Four minutes have elapsed. I continue with this procedure until all five fingers are crooked next to the palm. Then I allow those fingers to be free. By this time, ten minutes have gone by. Then I start using the other hand and continue in the same manner until all twenty minutes have elapsed. This procedure saves looking at the clock or watch.

What happens when meditating? Why does the beta state become the alpha or alpha/theta state? It's probably the deep restfulness of meditation. It's known that delta comes to us during the deepest restfulness of all, non-rem sleep.

Before the twenty minutes are over you'll discover that your breaths are quite shallow and regulated, and the heartbeats are slower. You'll find that your overall feelings are calm, and that probably you're in a serene state. You'll feel very rested. It has been shown that meditation will give you more rest than the equivalent time you spend in sleep.

Concentration. It's best if you can form a visual picture of each number while you're counting. Our brains will not produce a perfect picture of a number; the brain must be told what to look for. How can you concentrate on the number if it's a general blur? You tell your brain what you want to see. Here's an example:

Tell the brain/mind that the number one is one foot tall, four inches wide, with a horizontal line at the base and a small seraph at the left top. It's made of wood, a half inch thick, and is painted flat white. It stands on a table with a blackboard directly behind it.

Breaths number two to twenty-six will be the same size, the same painted color, standing on a table with the blackboard behind it.

You can change the color or design of the numbers one through twenty-six. I like firecrackers, so I imagine the numbers with those beautiful and powerful red cylinders and wicks. These are fitted close together and cover the entire number. You can do this with any item you desire. They could be apricots, figs, marbles, watch faces, tiny roses, dimes, etc. You can change the design after each set of twenty-six numbers, yet it's best to stick with one series for several minutes.

Types of numbers. We are most accustomed to numbers that are Arabic. You can switch off to Roman numbers; these are a delight to use. Lately, after many many years, I've been using the printed word for numbers (cardinal).

Letters. We count from one to twenty-six because the alphabet has twenty-six letters, and we can switch to using letters instead, from A to Z. So, all that has been said here about numbers applies to letters too. You can use capital letters, lower case letters, calligraphed letters. You can picture a blackboard and write the letter on the blackboard. You can visualize writing a letter on a yellow legal pad, a secretary shorthand pad, or scratch it in a damp clay tablet, and so on.

In conclusion, counting breaths is just one method of meditation. Originally, I used Le Shan's method and elongated it to twenty-six numbers. It works fine for me these many years. It's also an easy method or procedure to learn and to work with. I learned numbers as a child; later in life I studied calligraphy. Numbers are with us every day and with everything we do. I can visualize numbers very easily and change them around whenever I want. They can be white, (or any color), large or small, on a blackboard, or on the Hollywood Hills. I beckon them with my eyes closed. You can see more with your eyes closed than with your eyes open.

Studies of Meditation

In Herbert Benson's book *The Relaxation Response*, Dr. Benson is concerned with the medical side of meditation. His subjects are stress, lowering blood pressure, improving physical and emotional health. He writes about physiological functions controlled by the meditative techniques of Yoga and Zen Buddhism. Zen monks in Japan, while in meditation, can decrease oxygen consumption and therefore the metabolism faster than in sleep. He goes on to state that oxygen consumption, after four to five hours of sleep, decreases by about eight percent lower than when awake; while in meditation, the decrease is ten to twenty percent in the first three minutes.

Benson notes that there are 4 elements of meditation:

1. Quiet environment (turning off all internal and external stimuli).
2. An object to dwell on.
3. Passive attitude: empty all thoughts and distractions from the mind.
4. Comfortable position: firm enough to stay in for twenty minutes.

In David Goleman's book *The Meditative Mind*, he discusses the preparations for meditation. In ancient and medieval times there was an oral textbook on meditation, and monks memorized the contents.

The monks only had eight possessions:

3 robes

1 begging bowl

1 razor

1 sewing needle

Sandals

Food (in moderation).

Goleman surveys all phases of meditation: Hindu Bhakti, Jewish Kabbalah, Christian Hesychasm and nine other paths. He points out the history, people, methodology and beginning and ending results. His book is the most complete on the subject of meditation that this writer has found.

Israel Regardie has written a chapter on meditation within his book *Foundations of Practical Magic*. He strongly urges us to continue meditating until it works. He notes that one can distract oneself through meditation. For example, a toothache or other pain can be lessened. He states that we meditate to seek power, peace, reduce inner tension, develop creativity, and to review and realize the self. Physical relaxation is necessary. Let the mind roam over the body to become aware of minor discomforts and muscular tension. The body is to be in a relaxed state while, at the same time, the mind is wide-awake and vigilant. He talks of doubts and fears – and the ability to succeed. It's best to meditate in a room of your own. If meditation on your own doesn't work, then a teacher is needed. Don't eat before meditating; it's a disturbing factor; and is not conducive alertness, vigilance or enthusiasm. In sleep the ego is displaced and so is the perceived.

Salle Merrill Redfield, in the book, *The Joy of Meditating*, tells us that guided imagery can also place you within the state of serenity. Once in a relaxed state of mind and body, within your mind you walk up a nature trail. The trail takes you to a forest, a stream and green foliage all around. Here you find a place to sit and listen to the water, wind and animals. Try this for twenty minutes with eyes closed.

Recent brain studies provide new evidence of the benefits of meditation. The May 7, 2001 issue of *Newsweek Magazine* reports the new scientific discoveries in an article titled "God and the Brain." The article shows what happens to the brain when one is in deep prayer or deep meditation. The front page states, "How we're wired for spirituality."

It's stated that the rudimentary research in the 1950's and 1960's found that brainwaves change when you meditate. That research was silent on why brainwaves change, or which regions in the brain bring on these changes.

At the University of Pennsylvania, Dr. Andrew Newberg and Michael J Baime collaborated studying the "moment of peak transcendence" of Tibetan Buddhist meditation. Dr. Baime and seven other Tibetan Buddhist meditators went into the meditative state. When Dr. Baime knew he was at the peak – by special means of communication – he notified Dr. Newberg. Dr. Newberg then injected a radioactive tracer into an IV line that ran into Baime's left arm. By computer tomography they detected the tracer flow in the brain. The prefrontal cortex lit up. The bundle of neurons toward the top and back of the brain had gone dark. With the tracer, the areas of spiritual and meditational experiences can be pinpointed. For your reading on these concepts, see *Zen and the Brain*, by Dr. James Austin, published by M.I.T. Publishing (1998); *Varieties of Anomalous Experiences*, American Psychological Association; and *Why God Won't Go Away?* by Andrew Newberg (2001).

It's been stated that the main purpose of meditation is to put the diarist into a state of serenity. However, it must be stated here that there's much more to it than that. Other benefits are:

1. It allows you to set aside pain, (by distraction).

2. Helps you get into hypnogogic imagery.

3. When sleep won't come, it will make you drowsy and relaxed (and it'll then be easier to fall sleep).

4. Gives you rest and thus more energy.

5. When in meditation, and near or within alpha, a person can solve problems. Emanuel Swedenborg (1688-1772) used meditation to solve religious, scientific, and other problems. He was a Swedish scientist, philosopher and religious writer. In 1716, he distinguished himself by inventing machines for carrying boats inland from Stromstadt to Iddeljord. He devoted himself to scientific research and publishing his findings. In 1747, he resigned from his previous work and devoted himself thereafter to psychical and spiritual research. His followers constituted a considerable society, known as New Jerusalem Church.

   Swedenborg would meditate on ideas and problems related to inventing, writing, and for religious reasons. It was known that he could get into a deep state of meditation within less than five minutes. I taught at the University of San Fernando Law School. After a full day of practicing law, tired out, I would drive my car, park under a tree and meditate for half an hour. I felt renewed energy and calmness, thus ready to go back to work.

6. "Me time." Professor Nina Menrath of Sonoma State College, California, who taught diary writing, once told me that meditation allowed her to be alone with herself. She called it "Me time."

7. It gets you into the alpha state; once there, you can work on what you want. The unconscious has opened its door. With the door open, creativity flows. (Have you recorded this new creativity in your diary?)

8. It lowers blood pressure, shallows the breath.

9. While in hypnopompic reverie (twilight) state, count the numbers, and this will place you in lower twilight state.

10. Dialoguing can be used when in alpha (hypnogogic or hypnopompic). A man's face appears; i.e., you see the image of a face that you've never seen before in your life. Talk to the man. "Who are you?" He'll tell you. He may say that he's from Norway and he doesn't know why he's in your mind. Let him talk; egg him on. Later this can go into the diary and for future use.

Thus, you can see that meditation is a valuable practice.

<u>Hypnogogic Imagery.</u>

While in meditation you may get close to sleep. In this drowsed state images, sounds and the other senses may appear from their own source. (That is, without any use of your imagination or will. They simply come in without your asking them to. They're strong enough to stay in memory until you write them down or draw them out. This is where a great amount of creativity comes from. Remember –you're in meditation and so you're awake; these are not dreams (night or day-dreams). So be on the watch for them; they're a gift from the unconscious or other places. (This subject will be explored in detail in the next chapter.)

While meditating, a person may fall asleep. After all, the elements that go into sleep are all there: the eyes are closed and you're in a relaxed state. It's best just to continue meditating and get its benefits. In the event sleep is needed more than meditation, of course, then go to sleep.

If this chapter does not work for you (that is, after practicing you believe you have not gotten into the alpha state), then you may want to seek guidance. Because I believe the knowledge and use of meditation is so important in so many ways, I feel you ought to pursue the challenge. Almost every town in the United States has classes that teach meditation. For example in Santa Cruz, California, there are four meditation instruction centers: one Buddhist, one Christian, one "creative arts" and a Siddha Yoga Center.

Chapter 10

Dreams

Dreams come while you're asleep. When you lay your head on your pillow and lose consciousness, you're in the sleeping state.

The dreams you have while asleep are to be distinguished from daydreams, which are dreams you have while you're awake and the imagination takes over (perhaps with your eyes wide open). Everyone has experienced daydreams at various times in his or her life. Those who daydream a lot are called dreamers.

Daydreams must also be distinguished from hypnogogic and hypnopompic imagery. The former takes place while you are awake in a drowsy state just before sleep. Hypnopompic is similar to hypnogogic, except these images come after sleep and while you're awakening in the drowsy state. Some call this the twilight zone.

While you're asleep, you have little or no control of the dream's content. However, there are some theories today about how to control dreams. I believe that trying to control your dreams destroys their message, that our unconscious is enlightening the conscious mind or telling us something. After you've read this chapter, you'll see that I am against invading and destroying the spontaneity of our dreams. There is at least one exception, however: if you're having a nightmare and realize this while you're dreaming, then abort the dream.

Because this book is about diary techniques, we want to establish techniques for recording dreams.

To make sure you will have a dream tonight and record it, you might follow this suggestion. Take your diary book and open it to today's date. Write on that page, "*I shall have a dream tonight and I shall record it.*" Writing this in your journal is a suggestion to yourself, an affirmation (confirming that it will happen). The word "shall" is the strongest word for making something happen in the future. It's best that you write the sentence just before you turn out the light and place your head on the pillow.

Prior to going to bed, work out a system of where you will write if you wake up when it's dark and when the light is dim or bright. For those who sleep in a room where others are asleep as well, you'll want to write in another room so as not to disturb them. Thus, pick a place in another room, perhaps where there's a table or favorite chair. Have your diary book and pens at that spot or, if at your bedside, then take them with you.

If you wake in the middle of the night and a dream is in your mind, you may not know if it's important or not. Don't take the chance of believing it's not important, because it may be that the dream will help you understand what's troubling you now, giving you insight. Even if you're sleepy, record the dream. You'll be rewarded.

Once you're awake, and have a place to go to write, don't turn on any lights, for light will destroy the dream's content. Instead, *squint*. Keep your eyes closed except for a slit. Find your way to the other room. You'll have pre-arranged the lighting there. It's best to have a dimmer switch, where you can control the amount of light (adjust the light to where you can see the page when squinting).

Then when you record, write down all the facts of the dream. Read it over to determine if any facts were left out. Then go back to bed.

The next morning is the time to find out the meaning of the dream. You might ask yourself: "What is this language saying?"

Analyzing the Dream (Interpretation)

Some dreams are almost straightforward. Over twenty years ago, I was taking chemotherapy for cancer and was in a cancer support group. There were thirteen in our group with many kinds of cancer. Two women had double mastectomies. In my dream I entered an oily, slow moving, green train. Within the train there were stairs going down to a corridor. I went down and opened several doors. In one room was a beautiful woman. She wore a long, black, velvet gown with a light purple trim. The front of her dress revealed she was without breasts. To me, it did not matter. Here was one of the most beautiful women in the world.

Another door I opened revealed a carpet that covered most of the floor. Under the carpet were three large eggs the size of small children, with faces. They were very still, as if they were all asleep.

After I thought for a while, the only interpretation for the eggs became obvious: each represented the three chemicals I was taking.

The train represented the terrible journey I was on. It was a slow train; it would take a long time to heal.

I typed up this dream and took it to our support group and read it to them. It was later posted on the bulletin board. One of the women (with the double mastectomy), who was not going out with men, told me later that because of my dream she started to date again.

When the dream seems beyond your first or tenth attempt at interpretation, use the dialogue technique. See my dream, "Driving up a Hill," on page 72 under Chapter 10, Dialogues. The main characters in that dream were not my wife and children, they were the car and me. So I had a dialogue between the two of us: car and me. It solved the mystery of the dream. When I reflected upon the dream, it also said watch out for what you're doing. When money comes in, take a portion and save it. By experience you know there are good and bad financial times. Remember the economics class – take care of yourself.

Meditation

After meditating and in the alpha state (with eyes closed and little sound or light interfering); the mind, psyche, is clear and in a relaxed state. While in that state, it's easier to interpret a dream. Your imagination will help. What does it all mean? Does the dream reflect what has happened in the near or distant past?

Hypnogogic and hypnopompic states are a good place to be in for dream interpretation. In the former, you're drowsy, nearing sleep, and answers will come. The hypnopompic state is an even better place to be in because it lasts much longer. You can spread out the *twilight* for an hour or more if necessary. Matters fall into place. The dream the night before has recently happened and you can linger on it. Review each aspect of the dream: what place does it have in your life?; What answers and questions does it give you? Dialogue mentally.

After Analyzation

Write your analysis into your diary so you will have it. This part is just as important as the dream.

Mary Watkins, in her book *Waking Dreams* points out the subjective and objective method of analyzing dreams. Here's her example on page 129: a student dreams that his mother goes to the chairman of the academic department to apologize for the young man's work. After the dream, he begins to think about his mother's critical attitude toward him; how she sides with the forces he's having a hard time contending with. He begins an analysis on the *objective material* level, where images are equated with concrete reality. Jung understood that images also have a *subjective* level of significance. The mother is not just the biological mother but represents a part of the dreamer's personality.

You may want to look both outwards and inwards during your analysis of a dream.

Kilton Stewart was a member of a scientific group that traveled through the unexplored rain forest of the Malay Peninsula in 1935. He found a group of twelve thousand people living in a community among the mountains.

As a psychologist and writer, he was introduced to the isolated tribe of jungle folk who employed methods of psychology and interpersonal relations of astonishing magnitude.

These people, the Senoi, claim there has been no violent crime or inter-communal conflict for two to three hundred years.

Study of their society seems to show that they have arrived at a high state of social and physical cooperation – by using a system they invented and developed.

After a year of experience with these people, working as a research psychologist and another year in England integrating other studies, Stewart says: "I am able to make the formulations of the principles of Senoi psychology."

Senoi psychology falls into two categories: dream interpretations and, second, dream expression in the agreement trance or cooperation reverie.

Cooperative reverie is not participated in until adolescence and serves to initiate the child into the status of adulthood.

Dream interpretation is a feature of child education and common knowledge to all adults.

Breakfast in the Senoi house is like a dream clinic with fathers and brothers listening and analyzing dreams of children.

After breakfast, the males gather in a council, at which time the dreams of the older children – and all men of the community – are reported, discussed and analyzed.

This is their theory: man creates images of the outside world in his own mind. Some of these are in conflict with his dealings with others. Once internalized, these hostile images turn against himself and his fellows.

With the help of dream interpretation, the wasteful psychic, organic and muscular tension can be redirected and reorganized, and become useful to the dreamer.

Falling dream. When a Senoi child reports a falling dream, adults answer with enthusiasm. "That is a wonderful dream, one of the best a man can have. The falling spirit loves you. They are attracting you to their land." Over a period of time, social intercourse, praises, criticism, interpretation and advice, cause the fear of the falling dreams to change into the joy of flying. This happens to everyone in the Senoi society.

Love. When the dreamer demands and receives love, which he can express to the group on awakening, he realizes he cannot express or receive too much love in dreams.

In the _West_, however, the thinking we do while we sleep usually remains muddled, childish, or on a psychotic level because we do not respond to dreams as socially important. This social neglect, when the creative process is most free, seems to be poor education.

Since WWII, the Stewart article has been looked down on by a few skeptics. The Senoi suffered during WWII from deprivation and displacement. Nevertheless, there have been "Senoi dream workshops" used to this day.

In Lucia Capacchione's book _The Creative Journal_, she points out the following suggestions.

Drawing a dream

Draw the key images that appeared. These might be people, animals, objects and so on; even symbol forms.

Then write about the images in free-association (use the same page as the drawing for the text). What was the focus of the dream?

Then allow the images to speak (dialogue). This should be similar to a script for a play.

Pay attention to hunches and intuitions, and write them down. Make sure they are connected and apply.

Chapter 11

How to Find Your Hypnogogic Imagery

Recognizing

I didn't discover hypnogogic imagery until I was fifty-one years old. I was ripe for the experience. Not only was I slowing down in my law practice, but I also had taken the Ira Progoff course, *The Intensive Journal*, at UCLA. In this course, I had learned to meditate and to dialogue. Then I enrolled in a small class in diary writing with Tristine Rainer, who had recently finished her book, *The New Diary*. I was so fascinated by the subject that I had read and outlined her book before class met for its first session.

Early in the course, Ms. Rainer gave us an assignment for homework: write a paper describing the best time to write. I wrote on the subject, but Ms. Rainer and my fellow classmates criticized it. All the other students' papers were better than mine. Their papers seemed to have more imagination. But, undeterred, I continued my work in the course with enthusiasm. The whole world was my beat. Whatever was important to me, I would put in my diary.

However, something occurred one morning not long after the assignment that has since become an integral part of my diary writing. I woke briefly around four A.M. I was awake, waiting to return to sleep. My eyes were closed, and I was under the quilt relaxing when I saw and talked to a naked female, a girl with wings. She was one and a half inches in length. She was flying near me. Her winged motion was that of a hummingbird; she could fly and hover. When this one-and-a-half inch nude female, (beautiful insect, bird or angel) flew near my head, I spoke to her. I said, "When is the best time to write?" She flew to my right ear and held on to the top. Her wings stopped; she was not in motion.

She answered me in plain English, "The best time to write is when I bat my eyelashes, or when I say...Now! Or when I put my finger in your ear." Then she jumped into space and flew away.

I knew I was awake. I was not close to sleep. What had happened? This had never happened to me before. Was this a new phenomenon? I knew that I must discuss this phenomenon with Ms. Rainer.

At the next class meeting, I shared my experience with my instructor. "Tristine," I said, "I had a very special dream early Sunday morning, and I wrote it in my diary."

"Tell me about it." She said.

"Well, it was about four in the morning, quite cold, and I was under the quilt. I had returned from the bathroom, sleepy and ready to return to sleep."

"Yes, go on."

"I got back under the quilt, closed my eyes and was about to drift off. I knew I was not yet asleep. Then, while awake, a dream came to me. It was not a sleeping dream."

"Tell me the dream."

"I'll read it to you," I said, getting out my diary.

"No, let me read it." She took the diary from me, and read the entry. When she looked up, she said, "It has to do with a two-inch fairy visiting you and flying about your ear."

I nodded, "I don't know what this is. I didn't imagine this. I wasn't asleep."
I paused for a minute, and then I added, "I have named this phenomenon *quilted meditation.*"

Ms. Rainer laughed, and then smiled at me, "Ray, you gave it a good name, but this phenomenon already has a name. It's called *hypnopompic imagery.*"

"Where did you learn about it?" I asked.

"It came up in my class at the university. I have a book that explains it – I'll bring it next week."

In the next session, she brought the book, which included an entire chapter on the subject. Since that time, I've searched for other books dealing with the subject of *quilted meditation*. This is what I learned.

Understanding

Hypnopompic images come to the mind during awakening, that is, when coming out of sleep. If the images come just before sleep, they're called hypnogogic. The *Psychiatric Dictionary*, published by the Oxford University Press, defines hypnogogic imagery as occurring during the stage between wakefulness and sleep; that is, just before sleep has set in. Hypnopompic imagery is defined as the visions or mental pictures that occur just after the sleeping state and before full wakefulness. The phenomenon is analogous to hypnogogic imagery, save for the time at which the images occur. (For the sake of simplicity, throughout this chapter I shall refer to both types of images as "hypnogogic.")

Van Dusen, in his book *The Presence of Other Worlds*, says of the hypnogogic state that the normal findings are available to anyone who troubles to seek them, and they are simple and harmless. He further states that the hypnogogic state is one that is usually experienced by everyone twice a day, upon going in to and out of sleep. Awaking in the morning, or drifting back into sleep after waking, we can linger on the edge of inner imagery while being partially awake.

Only a small percentage of the population records even sleeping dreams, much less hypnogogic images. There are several reasons why these images are not important to people. Many believe that the images are nonsense and have no meaning in their lives. Most people experience hypnogogic images, but give them no credence. For instance, if the images emerge before sleep, you'll most likely put them aside and go to sleep, forgetting them forever. You may not care about the images, or they may have no value to you. Most likely, however, you're not even cognizant that they exist. In addition, if the images emerge just prior to waking, you'll most likely lose them through distraction – by opening the shades and looking at the sunrise, by turning on the lights, or by engaging in conversation. Many of us wake with important thoughts on our minds, plans for the day, which distract us from any hypnogogic images we've experienced.

Most people – even those with a great deal of education – have not heard of the term hypnogogic. Yet, for any person – a writer, sculptor, composer, bridge builder, doctor, teacher, engineer or anyone who wishes to acquire these images – they're extremely valuable. Hypnogogic images work in a special way as they spark creativity. The *unconscious* produces an *image* and the *conscious* receives it.

The conscious mind, while semi-awake, receives the image from the unconscious part of the mind. The image may be a picture, complete story, poem, song, invention or idea. The image may be incomplete. When the image is incomplete, the conscious mind is capable of completing it. Once recorded, the image stays and is yours forever.

One method of allowing the conscious mind to complete the image is to remain within the hypnogogic state (after awakening and in the twilight state), awake but not totally awake, and you can work in the following fashion. Keep your eyes closed, stay warm under the covers, and in your mind stay with the subject of the image. You only have part of the story, poem, picture. In your mindset, use both the conscious and unconscious to complete the story, pictures, poem or image. Such methods include dialoguing with characters, places, objects, ideas or with the unconscious itself.

Hypnogogic images have been discussed by scholars in many fields of study, such as: Professor McKim of Stanford University in his book *Experiences in Visual Thinking*; Mike Samuels and Nancy Samuels in *Seeing with the Mind's Eye*; Wilson Van Dusen in *The Presence of Other Worlds;* and Andreas Mavromatis in *Hypnagogia.* The concept of hypnogogic images as a creative force has been studied and used throughout history by such well-known figures as Thomas Alva Edison, Emanuel Swedenborg, Wilhelm Richard Wagner, Edgar Allan Poe and Charles Dickens.

I was lucky to find Poe's "Between Wakefulness and Asleep," which has had quite an impact on my connection to hypnogogic imagery. My wife Helen and I were in Philadelphia several years ago for a visit to relatives. While there, we also visited Poe's home. Poe had lived in Philadelphia from 1838 to 1844. The house where he, his wife Virginia and his mother-in-law lived is now operated by the Department of the Interior. They keep the house clean, show slides, give tours and sell Poe's books.

Edgar Allan Poe was born in 1809, and was orphaned at the age of two. When he was twenty, his foster mother died, and he became permanently estranged from his foster father, who admitted that he had never loved Poe. Poe's life was without money or love. However, he discovered that in his depression he could write. It was from this depression that he has left us such works as "The Raven," "Annabel Lee," "The Gold Bug," and "The Bells."

After touring the house, I purchased *The Portable Poe*, edited by Philip Van Doren Stern. I had read elsewhere that Poe had experienced hypnogogic images. The book did not contain an index, so I checked the table of contents, but found no clue under "Letters," "Fantasy," "Terror," "Death," "Revenge," "Murder," or "Poems." However, there it was under "Opinions," the essay, "Between Wakefulness and Sleep." That had to be it.

I read the essay, which was very flowery. Although the term *hypnogogic* was not yet a word or term, Poe used other terms to describe the same state: *fancy* and *psychol*. It appeared he had found the hypnogogic state and imagery. I felt sure that he had. Poe's terms stemmed from his reasoning that the imagery comes not from thought, but from "fancy." The "fancies" were not intellectual, but psychological, thus psychol. He elaborated that these images came to him when he was startled into wakefulness. He also suspected that this phenomenon did not apply to him alone, but was common. He wrote about his enjoyment while in the hypnogogic state, the happiness and serenity he experienced.

Although I've not found evidence to establish which of Poe's writings stem from his "fancies," I know by my own experience that both entire stories and poems, as well as fragments of such, can come from hypnogogic imagery. Mr. Stern notes, in his introduction to *The Portable Poe*, that Poe "tapped the rich reservoir of the subconscious mind to set free the strange and terrible images which had seldom been allowed to stalk the printed page." My guess would be that such a work as "The Raven," because of its odd state of affairs, was at least partly inspired by "fancy" from Poe's unconscious. I can imagine Poe in bed, on his back, drifting toward sleep, and then experiencing a startle – an involuntary awakening – leading to a significant discovery: he wasn't asleep, and yet he had this imagery, this "fancy". And we have the benefit of being able to read recorded versions of those images.

We also have the benefit of reading the writings of Emanuel Swedenborg, the great scientist and theologian. To solve problems and to ponder the mysteries of religion, Swedenborg would place himself in a hypnogogic state by way of meditation. He recorded the results in his dream diary and a five-volume spiritual diary. His practice of Hindu Yoga allowed him to slow down his breathing as a part of directing his concentration inward.

Other writers have expressed that the twilight state exists on both sides of sleep, and some writers describe these states as hypnogogic zones. Sigmund Freud stated that the royal road to our unconscious is through our sleeping dreams. However, they only occur when we're asleep. Like dreams, hypnogogic images come to us unexpectedly, and therefore are beyond the control of our conscious minds. In this way, they're similar to sleeping dreams. These images, like sleeping dreams, come from our unconscious. There are several ways to uncover the unconscious, and hypnogogic imagery is one.

Here's an illustration that combines the concepts of hypnogogic imagery and the twilight state. At three in the morning, you lie awake under the covers, and you receive a picture-image of the head and face of a gray granite statue. That's all you perceive. You get out of bed and record, composing as you talk to the image (dialogue) and it talks back to you. As you do this, you remain in the twilight state, partially because you use little light and you're squinting. Your thoughts are dreamy and imaginative, totally different from those of your waking hours – perhaps even poetic. Later you will find that trying to correct, rewrite and amend this writing while fully awake (in the beta state) will not work. You must be in the same mental state as you were during its recording.

Creating (Inventing)

I fish the ocean, this is my fishing ground. I put my line, sinker and hook over the side of the boat.

My dad says, "Let the sinker go to the bottom and then come up six inches."

"What's down there, Dad?"

"Oh, sand dabs, halibut. But, my son, you never know what you will bring up."

My first hook up was a small rubber boot. Then a mackerel, then seaweed was hooked. Of course, in different fishing grounds there are different species. The unconscious is my new fishing ground. You never know what is there and what might come out.

Hypnogogic images come to us automatically. We don't see them swimming in a tank. In our unconscious state, we have no control over what comes out. It's the thrill of the unknown that makes me smile and say "thank you." I'll trade the small rubber boot for an image of Anne Frank.

It's my opinion that poetry, stories and all creativity coming from the unconscious is superior to what comes from the conscious mind. I'm constantly reminded that my unconscious self is a better writer than my conscious self. (See my two stories of Anne Frank, one from my beta or conscious mind, and the other from alpha or the unconscious mind.) Over the years, I've written poetry from my conscious state. Recently, poetry has come from the hypnogogic state, and I've found that it's much better than the poetry that comes from the conscious state.

Why is this? The conscious mind is constantly distracted. Even in a quiet place, the eardrums are constantly receiving messages, sometimes pounding with vibrations that are channeled into the brain. While working with the conscious mind, the writer must see, feel, hear and taste in order to write, but must do so synthetically, through the conscious memory.

During the experience of hypnogogic imagery, the subject's eyes are closed; the atmosphere is generally quiet and dark. The outside elements of light, sound and other distractions are not dulling the mind. There's no sense of an audience, no feeling of being monitored by a critic. The image comes fast without thought of revision, without consideration of "good" or "bad." The image isn't synthetic, but immediate. The result is a message, which is free and flows directly without interruption.

From the unconscious mind comes its own rhythm. Later, the conscious mind may look back and discover the source.

The unconscious is a storehouse. Goleman, Kaufman and Dutton, in their book *The Creative Spirit*, explain that everything we know is in the unconscious. Information that flows through the brain, and *all* memory, is within the unconscious before it becomes conscious. Less than one percent reaches conscious awareness. The unconscious is richer; it has more data to draw on. The authors go on to explain that it's at the point of "letting go" that creativity occurs. Falling asleep, performing repetitive tasks, dreaming, waking up, showering and meditating, are all examples of times when we're letting go of our analytical side and allowing creativity to occur. In such situations, as Lester Sdorow explains in his book *Psychology*, there's a unique state of physical and mental relation in which alpha brain waves are increased, and the heart rate, respiration rate, oxygen consumption, and carbon dioxide expiration are decreased. This physical state allows the unconscious to function entirely in a different way.

Such authorities as Freud and Jung have placed a great deal of emphasis on the unconscious, pointing out that, for instance, the unconscious childhood experiences stored in the brain continue to affect us without our conscious awareness of them. Jung goes further to explain his belief that there is a personal unconscious and a collective unconscious. The collective unconscious contains inherited memories passed down from generation to generation. These memories are archetypes representing important aspects of the accumulated experience of humankind. It's his opinion that there's no knowledge of how the unconscious functions, and that, as an independent system, it may contain all that the conscious has experienced, including perception, memory, apperception, imagination, will, effectivity, feeling, reflection and judgment – all in subliminal form. Jung admitted the plausibility of Freud's assertion that dreams are the mediators of such unconscious contents.

When images, sounds, words and other sensory objects come into our conscious minds, and are not *willed* from our conscious mind, then these objects can be said to come from "another place." The unconscious mind has saved these images from its own vast collection, a collection that includes all the forgotten matter of the conscious mind, and perhaps even matter from a collective unconscious. Hypnogogic imagery is an avenue, or tool, by which we allow the unconscious to enrich the conscious. The twilight state itself is not a state of the unconscious. It is a state in which the hypnogogic resides, and from which the hypnogogic filters information from the unconscious to the conscious.

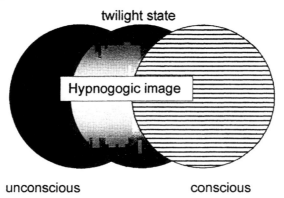

twilight state

Hypnogogic image

unconscious   conscious

The value of hypnogogic imagery, in all its various forms, is its creative aspect. This creative aspect feeds the work of writers, painters, philosophers, builders, accountants, physicians – anyone who will allow the images to be recorded. Who would not enjoy receiving a poem, story or idea from his or her own *l'autre moi* (alter ego) or unconscious? There are new rhythms, new emotions, original words and pictures from the hypnogogic state. In addition, there are new versions of old ideas, which take the form of hypnogogic images, as well. Don't be surprised if the version from the unconscious outdoes your conscious creativity.

The unconscious has more to work with than the conscious. Yet the conscious, we think, has more control. However, some psychologists believe that the unconscious has overall control. For our purposes – for invention – let the unconscious give us what it wants.

The unconscious has your whole self from which to work. Its tools are your personality, your memory, your skills, your emotional makeup and all the rest that composes you. Your unconscious will not conjure up words and images that apply to someone else. It can only work with what's uniquely yours. If you're a potter, your unconscious contains the whole of your memory and training. It knows of your special ideas, of your talented hands, even your temper. If you can still your mind by meditation before or after sleep, the unconscious may offer creative advice. It may produce ideas, pictures and words that can result in an original creative endeavor. If you're a business executive, your unconscious contains the whole of your memory and training, as well. It knows your managerial techniques, your skills at negotiating, your approach to project development. Your unconscious may offer you creative advice that can result in new ways to deal with business situations. Whether you're an artist or an artisan, a sculptor or a real estate agent, hypnogogic imagery can provide a new source for ideas.

Hypnogogic imagery can be used as a form of invention once it's recognized. However, it's a discovery that only you can make for yourself. Once you've mastered the skills required to record such images, you'll find that the phenomenon is another source of creativity – for new ideas, word combinations and poetry. In fact, upon reading the recorded images, you will undoubtedly be surprised, and might think: "Why, I couldn't possibly have written this. It's not part of me." What's more, no matter how many hypnogogic images you record, you will probably be surprised and delighted with each one. However, you must realize that these images come from the unconscious. If you intentionally try to usher them in, they won't come. Part of the appeal of these images is that they move toward you unannounced, and they resist control. In other words, hypnogogic images are autonomous and they are uncontrollable. The power of the holder is to wait for them, to stay alert, and then to allow them to make a good impression on the memory and then record them.

In order to record the images so that they remain in their pure state, you must do so under certain conditions. These conditions are described on the following pages.

Recording

A person who has received hypnogogic imagery will want to preserve the experience. It may be a fine poem or it may be the start of a new invention, the solution to a problem, a musical composition, a new idea for the sculptor, potter or writer. Don't allow it to slip away, *record it*.

In order to receive the value of hypnogogic imagery, you'll have to earn it. That means that you must become knowledgeable about the phenomenon. You must learn the rules that will give you the imagery:

1. Learn how to relax your body and mind.

2. Be alert as to the possibility of receiving an image.
3. Learn to recognize the image.
4. Know the appropriate setting for recording images.
5. Be motivated to record the image.

These rules are relatively simple. Each one requires special consideration, however, and what follows is a detailed explanation of each.

1. Learn how to relax your body and mind.

Your first task in receiving hypnogogic images is to learn how to relax your body and mind. For example, a carefree vacation is a fertile time to receive images. I have had this experience myself. My wife, Helen and I took a weekend vacation to Ojai, California, an easy drive from our home in Los Angeles. As a lawyer, my worries of a lawsuit were left at home and office.

The room in which we stayed offered a bed that was high off the floor; we needed a small ladder to reach the top. In the middle of one of the nights there, I awoke, went to the bathroom, returned, found the ladder and got back into bed. I was very relaxed and wanted to go back to sleep. I was drowsy, but awake. I was very close to being asleep when a hypnogogic image came my way. I didn't think it important to record, as sleep was calling, and I believed the story was not very important. Yet, I got up anyway and wrote it out entirely. After waking in the morning and reading it, I was more than surprised; I was delighted. I showed it to Helen, who said the writing was my best ever. I said to myself, "I did not write this. I just recorded what I perceived. These images did all the bidding." This hypnogogic writing, *Fight for Life*, is included at the end of this chapter.

A key technique for relaxation is the ability to meditate. Mediation is an effective way to get into the serene twilight state. Mediation is not necessary to achieve hypnogogic imagery, but it can be a great help. (See the chapter on Meditation.)

The benefits of meditation include:

1. You are in the twilight state.
2. You are calm.
3. You are rested.
4. You are more prone to receiving hypnogogic imagery.

2. Be alert as to the possibility of receiving an image.

One of the key factors in achieving hypnogogic imagery is to learn to be alert while you are in a sleepy state. Sounds like an oxymoron? Yes. But it's possible to be alert in a sleepy state. You can control your mind to do so. Make it important to you so that you catch the imagery. Remember that it's the gold ring on the merry-go-round, it's hooking the yellowtail, it's being dealt the Jack to an inside straight. Tell yourself you want that gold ring.

Granted, being both relaxed and alert is a difficult state to achieve. The closer you are to sleep (whether waking from it or going into it), the more likely you are to experience a hypnogogic image. However, many people cannot stop from going into sleep, and they lose any images they may have had. Some people have a natural "startle" at the end of a hypnogogic image, which shakes them awake and allows them to record. Although Thomas Alva Edison was extremely aware, he had to create his own "startle." He sat prepared in his rocking chair, his head resting and feet on the floor, with two pie pans on the floor, one under each hand and in each hand he held several one-half inch steel balls. He knew that when he started to nap, he had little self-control and would go into sleep. But he "set a trap" for himself. At the start of sleep, his hands would relax and drop the steel balls, which caused a high-frequency bang that, even with his poor hearing, would awaken him, allowing him to retain the hypnogogic image from his twilight state.

As I've mentioned, alertness is near to the last link in the chain to acquiring the images. You should know that the phenomenon does not work if you are, first, extremely tired or sleepy, or second, under heavy stress. The best situation for receiving these images is that of total relaxation of both the body and mind. Also, I've found the following technique conducive to receiving images. As you lie down for sleep, under your breath whisper, "I will see or hear the images tonight (or this afternoon)." It really works. I taught a class in diary writing at the University of California at Santa Cruz. I wanted my students to learn the technique. I spent a lot of time explaining hypnogogic imagery. Then I gave the class a homework assignment: Acquire one of these images and bring back the written material to the class. They had one week to do this. Most of the class successfully completed the assignment.

3. Learn to recognize the image.

Although most people have never heard of hypnogogic images and never consciously experienced them, they are, I've found, very important and useful. In fact, I'm amazed to experience this state without having read about it, or having had any teacher tell me about it. I believe that in order to have these experiences, it's crucial to be aware that they exist and to learn how to recognize them.

I will assume you're now aware of and believe in the existence of hypnogogic images through your reading thus far, even though you may have no memory of ever receiving them. In order to acquire them, you must realize that awareness alone is not enough, or at least won't do the job completely. To do the complete job, you need to be alert near the period of their occurrence, and recognize them as they come.

Remember, hypnogogic images – pictures or sound, in color or not – come to us just before sleep envelops us, or just as we're coming out of sleep. So, when you get into bed, or recline in your favorite chair or divan, and you're getting to the place where you almost fall into sleep, be alert for the images. Or, when you find yourself coming out of sleep, slow down a bit and relax, and be aware of any images that may be occurring. The image you experience may only be aural. Someone may talk to you; or, you may hear the sound of a waterfall, or a voice singing. There are many kinds of sounds you might experience. Visuals may be like still pictures, in black and white or in color. They may be pictures of people you've never seen. Since they come from your unconscious, they're yours. They may have value; they may give you an entire story, or ideas for a story or drawing, or something to ponder in your line of work.

How long do hypnogogic images last in our memory? It depends on the individual. It's fair to say that your conscious memory will retain such images at least until you're out of bed and sitting down to write. However, there are exceptions. For instance, if you turn on a bright light that shines in your eyes, then these images usually vanish.

4. Know the appropriate setting for recording images.

First, the best place to record twilight writing is in a hardcover diary book, which creates a feeling of permanence. The entries in the diary book seem to work best if arranged chronologically. However, whatever you choose to write in, it's more important that you take into account the atmosphere, which surrounds you.

Generally, there are a few key items concerning setting that you should know about that will allow you to most effectively record your hypnogogic images. First, if it's the middle of the night, don't turn the light on. Wake up easily and stay relaxed; don't wake your partner. Go into another room, keeping your eyes closed except for a small slight squint from one eye. While you're at the bed, chair or wherever you choose to record, *help the memory.* Know in your heart that the image is so precious that you'll hold it calmly in your memory until it's written down. Remind yourself that the images from the unconscious can help you write, invent, compose, sculpt or work with your inner self. These are precious gems; don't lose them.

Keep in mind that only a very low light should be behind you. The low light allows you to see the page, but it should never reach your eyes directly. You should be able to see the paper, pen and the writing, even though your eyes are not fully open. Write or draw freely, recording the images from beginning to end. When you've finished, it's not necessary to read what you wrote at this time.

If you experience images *before* going to sleep or while meditating, it's very important that these are recorded. You're lucky if you have "the startle," which will awaken you, leaving you with a usually agreeable and pleasant feeling. There are, perhaps, more obstacles to recording images that come to you prior to napping than there are obstacles that come to you in the twilight state between sleeping and waking. These images often occur during the daytime, and the sun shining in a window or artificial light can be a distraction. If this occurs, close your eyes and face away from the light, or shade your eyes with your hand. Choose a low-lit area in which to record. Also, avoid becoming distracted by anyone who's attempting to engage you in a conversation. Don't allow anything to disrupt your process.

If you do allow the disruption, the imagery will probably disappear. The conscious mind is strong and will push the images aside. When Samuel Taylor Coleridge was recording images of Xanadu for "Kubla Kahn," a person knocked at his door. He went to the door and spoke to the person. When he returned to write again, the rest of the images were gone from his memory. Only those recorded images remained for himself and all humankind.

When dozing, the fact that you may not be in the best environment to record a hypnogogic image should not stop you from recording it. If you start to fall asleep in a beach chair while facing the sun, even with a startle there is little or no chance of retaining the imagery, because sunlight will destroy it. But, if you're under an umbrella, wearing a hat and sunglasses, keep your pen and paper handy.

Although many of us are prone to dozing on airplanes, it's even more difficult to record aboard an aircraft. In a narrow seat surrounded by passengers on all sides, with the constant roar of engines and vibrations to seat and floor, and sun shining in through windows, even if images come, it will be difficult to retain them long enough to record them. Recording might be easier with earplugs and a sleeping mask. Finally, keep in mind while you're recording that you must maintain objectivity; write down the image as it comes to you, with no interpretation. Later, you can rewrite and polish the image into whatever you wish it to be.

5. Be motivated to record the image.

One of the strongest motivational factors in achieving a good recording of a hypnogogic image is your sense of its usefulness. The whole concept of hypnogogic imagery should be important to you because the material is yours and no one else in the world has it. It's your monopoly and hence has great value.

I've included some examples of my own hypnogogic images. They take many forms, but all came from my unconscious. They're examples of how the unconscious mind can, given the right circumstances, provide source material for ideas – in this case writing.

_____

Five examples of Hypnogogic Imagery writing continue on the following pages.

Example 1

A Room in an Annex

Author's Note: In the fall of 1981, my wife, Helen, and I came from London, by air, to Amsterdam. Our main purpose was to see the Anne Frank House. From our hotel clerk we received the address and instructions. It was a short walk to the tramline. We boarded the narrow, high, yellow streetcar, which took us two streets from the Secret Annex. The annex, we found, faced a canal and a narrow street.

We opened the door, and were welcomed in and told we could give a donation for a ticket, or not – it was up to us. I happily gave the donation. We had the choice of waiting for a tour or going alone. Helen found the famous stairs, where the bookcase hid the occupants from view. Now the bookcase, on hinges, is left open at all times for the tens of thousands of visitors each year who go up those steps.

The steps were steep. Above, we found several rooms, including, finally, Anne's. It was a small room. There were three walls, and where the other wall would be was a narrow bed, a chair, and a table, on which sat a candle. Hanging on the wall to our left, we saw five posters advertising American films of the 1940's.

I started feeling squeamish and in need of air. We walked back down to the first level. Near the entrance was a shop, where two different posters were for sale – one, a picture of Anne and the other, a surrealist painting of death and life. I purchased the latter. In front of me was a very long row of books in a specially made case. The case was about thirteen feet long and held the books at an angle. I could see the spines just by looking down. I picked up several of these books. Each book was the same, except each had been printed in a different language.

Fifty-two books of the Anne Frank diary and fifty-two separate languages. All these countries have her diary.

As I was handling these books, two German men in their early twenties wearing trench coats gruffly came through the doorway from the outside and proclaimed that Anne Frank never existed, and that the Secret Annex was all a hoax.

The clerk behind the counter called for the police and for the men who were working behind the building.

One of the German men tore a picture of a concentration camp from the wall, yelling, "Where did you get this? You believe this? The Jews are the reason for all the world's ills!"

I thought, "Where is my rifle – get me a club – is this 1945 or 1981? Joseph Goebbels is dead, but his big lie remains in German and Austrian minds."

Finally, two workmen arrived with a hammer and a hatchet. They ordered the two German men to get into a corner until the police arrived.

Helen and I made our way back to the hotel. We could not believe what had just happened. "What did forty thousand American soldiers die for?" I asked, "We certainly did not completely stop the menace."

In the late afternoon, Helen and I went window-shopping. When it started to rain, we ducked under an awning. Two doors from us we saw a wax museum. Helen suggested, "Let's go in and spend an hour and maybe the rain will disappear."

"Okay," I said. "But I've seen a wax museum before and it didn't hold my attention."

There were strings of small white lights on the outside of the building. A barker in clown's uniform was asking everyone who passed to enter and see more than the spectacular. I paid the admittance fees, and received the tickets. An usher tore our tickets in half and asked us to move inside.

We walked in. Heavy, deep carpets cushioned our steps. The first group of figures was from the 1940s. General de Gaulle looked down from his height as if speaking to the figure of Winston Churchill. Franklin Delano Roosevelt, looking pleased but very old, sat in his wheelchair. All three were life-size. I was waiting for an eye to move.

Helen was just as impressed as I. "It takes a lot of know-how, talent, art and the knowledge of chemistry to make these figures," she said.

Each exhibit was better than the one before. Of course, Jack the Ripper and Bluebeard had their scenes.

We reached the third and final floor. There we found a room in front of us with one tiny light seemingly coming from the top of a candle. As we entered the room, Helen and I both stopped when we realized where we were. It was Anne Frank's room in the Secret Annex. It was night. The small light at the top of the candle was the flame that shone on Anne Frank; she was real. Her eyes were open. She looked like her photographs. She was not beautiful. Combed, dark hair lay close to her neck and shoulders. Her arms were bare and thin. She wore a plain dress. She sat at the table. Her face was composed in relaxed contemplation. A pen was in her right hand. Her diary lay on the table, held there by her left hand. She did not blink.

Tears came down my face. Helen was upset and also crying. Anne Frank was just far enough from us so that we couldn't touch her.

What follows is a hypnogogic image that came my way several years after the preceding experience.

Helen and I are in Amsterdam, mainly to see the Anne Frank House. It's the fall of 1981. We get a hotel across the street from the Rijks Museum. The room is half below ground level. The sun comes in and we have sights under ladies' dresses; the sight from my bed is better than the museum. We get instructions from the clerk to get to the Anne Frank House. We walk to Main

Strasse and then take yellow streetcars.

When we arrive – next to a canal – I am ready to ring the doorbell, when on the balcony a very fat man in a white military uniform and hat (I whisper to myself, "That's the Nazi Hermann Goring!") says, "Can I help you?"

"Yes. My wife, Helen, and I want to see the Anne Frank House."

Hearing me, he laughs great belly laughs, and then he says, "My good man, don't you know there's a war going on?"

"No, what war?"

He's bathing in laughter. He disappears and another officer appears. "What seems to be the trouble?"

"I know you – you're Adolf Hitler."

"That is true. What is it that you want?"

"My wife, Helen, and I want to see the Anne Frank House."

"Well, why don't you try the door knob?"

I open the door. Inside is the Luftwaffe command room, with its large maps, telephones, table with a scale model, microphones and speakers. From the speaker a pilot says, "Bombs are being dropped on London." Then the loud speaker reports that London is on fire.

A whole new scene appears: a long, narrow table, and seated facing us, with their backs to the wall, are three distinguished men – Franklin Delano Roosevelt, Stalin and Churchill.

FDR says, "Can I help you?"

"Sure, what are you drinking?"

"You wouldn't like it."

"Why?"

"Because it's wax."

"Wax?"

"Did you come to see the Anne Frank House?"

"Yes, we did." I am about to introduce Helen to FDR, but standing in her place and on two feet is the Statue of Liberty. I know it's Helen because the statue is purple, her favorite color.

FDR says, "It won't take long to see the house, but the main action is at the house known as the Wax Museum." Old FDR is right.

Outside, walking to the Wax Museum, Helen is still in the purple Statue of Liberty, and we walk through the brothel area. I wonder if FDR meant this kind of action.

We enter the wax museum. People are examining Helen for her wax. There's FDR in a wheelchair, and de Gaulle and Churchill immersed in Allied strategy. Helen and I walk by, since the three do not want to be disturbed.

In half an hour, we get to the third floor. Patrons try to blow out the torch in Helen's hands. We find ourselves going into a semi-dark room.

A young woman sitting at a table in very dim light says, "My name is Anne Frank. I'm writing my diary, but I am now at your service." She loved Helen's costume and wondered if we'd come from a dance.

"FDR said there's a lot of action here."

"Oh, no – not in this room."

"What goes on here?"

"Oh, it's mainly dipping my pen in an inkwell, letting the ink fall on the paper, and then repeating the process."

"Is that all that happens here?"

"You promise you will not tell anyone?"

"Of course."

"Well, on Saturday nights I leave this room, including the diary, pen, and inkwell."

"Where do you go?"

Helen, very curious, says, "Yes, where do you go?"

"Helen, you have the bluest eyes I have ever seen. Ray, have you always had a beard?"

"My beard is not important compared to your Saturday nights."

"Well – it's your beard! I will not tell you; you have upset me."

"Please," Helen and I both beg.

"All right.   Saturday nights, one hour after closing, all of us here go dancing on the main floor. This is secret information, understand?"

"Yes, we both understand."

"Today is Saturday. If you'll come back at one-thirty in the morning, I'll open the door for you. I'm sure Mr.-*oh-General* de Gaulle will want to dance with you, Helen, as the Statue of Liberty. I'll keep one dance especially for you, Ray."

The End

Example 2

Get Up You Bum

The action takes place one day in Jerusalem, in the second century, B.C. On two rocks sit two men, Ray and Bert.

RAY

Get up, you bum.

BERT

Who are you calling a bum? A bum is one who cannot earn a living.

RAY

Well!

BERT

Hey, cut it out. I have money in my pocket.

RAY

I bet not much.

BERT

Two shekels.

RAY

Let me see.

BERT

You don't trust anyone.

RAY

That's right.

BERT

I'll piss on your grave.

RAY

I'm to be cremated.

BERT

Mated with who?

RAY

Aw, shut up.

BERT

If I weren't so tired, I'd kick the stuffing out of you.

RAY

You're all talk.

BERT

Ray, I'm hungry.

RAY

What can we do about it?

BERT

The next big wench that comes by with groceries – I'll tackle and you grab the

food.

RAY

It's too risky.

BERT

All right. We'll wait for night. But I can't wait that long. Don't you have any food

on you?

RAY

Whee whee – hoota hoota.

BERT

What's that?

RAY

That's me – steam-letting.

BERT

Shorka shorka – bulla bue. That's my steam.

RAY

Don't lie in the street.

BERT

You can sit, since you have a fat rear.

Enter Sophie.

SOPHIE

Well, what do you bums have to say for yourselves?

BERT

Cut the crap; what do you have to eat?

RAY

We're starving.

SOPHIE

So? What else is new?

BERT

Sophie, I'm desperate.

SOPHIE

Aren't all beggars?

RAY

I know a wealthy one.

SOPHIE

That's a laugh. How would you both like a pork shank?

RAY

I'd rather die first; you know we're Jewish.

BERT

I could eat it and then die happily.

SOPHIE

Are you up to traveling four blocks for a good cooked meal?

RAY

It might take all evening – no, honestly, I could not make it.

BERT

I think I'd rather stay here and die.

SOPHIE

If I make dinner and breakfast will you work for me?

BERT

What kind of work?

SOPHIE

Garden work.

RAY

Bert, it's much easier to die.

Wait a minute, wait a minute. You have a big tub and clothes from your deceased

husband. We could look healthy and prosperous.

SOPHIE

How would you pay for them?

BERT

We could steal, rob, pick pockets.

SOPHIE

Hey, wait. I'm a law-abiding woman.

RAY

I'll just stay here and beg.

BERT

That's the easier way, for sure.

SOPHIE

If you change your minds, you know where my house is.

Sophie exits.

RAY

What are we going to do, Bert?

BERT

I don't know. Use your own head.

RAY

I ask a question, and I get an arrow in the neck.

BERT

Ray, we're in bad shape.

RAY

If we don't get food, death will have us for dinner.

BERT

Let's think. Any relatives, friends, others with food in Jerusalem?

RAY

Only Sophie.

BERT

Yeah. It may be our only chance.

RAY

With two meals and some work, it may just turn us around.

BERT

It's only four blocks.

RAY

We'll make it.

BERT

We can die in the effort.

RAY

Push me up and I'll pull you up.

BERT

Be careful, I hurt all over.

RAY

Oh! I fell back down.

BERT

Well, try again.

RAY

My knee is bleeding, but only slightly.

BERT

I told you to be careful.

RAY

You're larger than me, so be careful; we both may fall back. Up you goooo!

BERT

Steady – my knees and legs are shaking.

RAY

You should have sandals, like me.

BERT

Nah. Bare feet have been with me all the days of my life.

RAY

Lock arms.

BERT

Gotcha.

RAY

Short steps.

BERT

Slower.

RAY

I need a rest.

BERT

We've come only thirty steps.

RAY

You go ahead, Bert.

BERT

I won't leave you, Ray.

RAY

Go and get Sophie's wheelbarrow and come back for me.

BERT

Ray, I could not make it.

RAY

I need a little rest, and then I can go ahead.

BERT

Just rest. I'll sit on this rock.

RAY

Do you think I'll die tonight?

BERT

Of course not.

RAY

I'm not sure.

BERT

Just rest and then we will make it.

RAY

Okay.

Later that same day in Jerusalem, Ray and Bert awaken. It is night.

BERT

Wake up. It's time to walk to Sophie's for a hot meal.

RAY

Bert, I'm ready to die.

BERT

Give me your hand.

RAY

Back on my feet, Bert.

BERT

Let's go at least another thirty feet.

RAY

One step at a time.

BERT

The moon is out, and it's almost full.

RAY

Easier to find our way.

BERT

Make each step easy.

RAY

How much further?

BERT

Ray, just concentrate on each step.

RAY

How beautiful the night.

BERT

Oh, yes.

RAY

Silver clouds.

BERT

Slanted mountains.

RAY

Lights, candles.

BERT

Yes, I know. It's Sabbath. It's Friday night.

RAY

We should be inside.

BERT

A wife to help with the prayer over bread and wine.

RAY

Are we getting closer?

BERT

Of course.

RAY

I hear my maker calling me.

BERT

Just a dream.

RAY

I'm getting weaker.

BERT

I'll hold you.

RAY

Let me go to the ground.

BERT

How are you doing?

RAY

I'm serene.

BERT

I'll stay with you, buddy.

RAY

Good-bye Bert, my dear friend.

The End.

Example 3

Fight For Life

I walked out of the Roosevelt Hotel at Fifth and Main to take a smoke. Facing me on the sidewalk was a woman. Three men in trench coats stood behind her. She said that she expected me to be in the ring at the Olympic Auditorium at eight o'clock that evening. Then each of the three men (her seconds) handed me his business card: Hitler, Tojo and Mussolini.

At eight o'clock that night, I found myself in the ring at the Olympic, wearing boxing shoes, trunks and red leather gloves.

Across the ring stood this woman, wearing boxing shoes, trunks, a special brassiere with aluminum cups, and red leather gloves. In the center of the ring was God, as referee.

In the audience on her side sat part of the Sixth Corps of German soldiers who died at Stalingrad, many of the Japanese soldiers who died at Guadalcanal, and the Italian Mafia from New York and Chicago.

On my side of the audience sat the graduating class of Winter '43 from Franklin High School, many of my relatives and friends, a portion of the World War II Third Army with General George S. Patton cheering them on, the bluebird that flew into the window of the synagogue at my Bar Mitzvah, and FDR holding Fala on his lap.

The bell sounded and the referee (God) motioned us to the center. I said to God, "Who is this woman?" The woman told me that her initials were B.A.

I said, "What does it mean?"

"I'll tell you after the first knockdown."

God said, "Protect yourselves at all times, don't hit on breaking clinches. May the best person win."

We retreated to our corners, and then came out to fight each other. Studying for the Bar did not train me to box, thus B.A. had the advantage. We were somewhat cautious, until suddenly she lashed out and connected with a haymaker. I found myself on the canvas, with God counting over me. The round (year) was coming to an end and my seconds (wife and parents) carried me to the corner. I was in terrible condition, so they called a doctor. He performed electroshock therapy and, in just a little while, I was ready to resume the fight.

Getting out for round two, B.A. told me what her initials stood for: "Bipolar Affective." All I could think of was that she was part polar bear.

She said, "Goddamnit, you know nothing. It's the new term for manic depression."

"Screw you!" I said. "Let's fight!"

For the next five rounds (years) I had things my way. I could hit her at will. I broke her cheekbone, bloodied her right eye and her nose. The best part was when I caved in one of her aluminum cups.

In round six she got lucky, and her right glove connected with my chin. My seconds dragged me to the corner. The doctor said, "No more electroshock. We now have a pill – it's called lithium." The doctor whispered to me, "O.K., with the pill, the mania (middle to high) will be gone."

God brought us together – B.A., our seconds and me. He said, "It's no use recording each round, as the fight will continue to the end of your life. Only step into the ring when necessary. Make it as few times as possible."

The End

Example 4

Collecting Acorns

It's below ground; people are placing acorns to be used for food at a later time in neat, long, flat boxes. Mr. Pepys finds fat acorns, and is sliding them in neat rows. Mr. Emerson is pushing his into place with a short ruler. They're sprouting, and these he will share with the world. Virginia Woolf needs hers now, since food is scarce in World War I. Louisa May Alcott watches Emerson and her father, and she will also collect some day. Anne Frank collects a lot, but they'll be used by others. *

The End

---

*In this image, there's a central squirrel metaphor. Those who appear in the image are behaving as squirrels, hiding their food for the winter, for another time. The long, narrow boxes symbolize diaries. Pepys' acorns are fat to resemble him. The fact that he organizes them in neat rows shows his personality – he treated his books and code that way. Emerson's short ruler symbolizes his sense of measure – his diaries were indexed. His sprouting acorns are words that he used in his essays and lectures. Louisa May Alcott was helped by her famous father and by Emerson – through their examples she would later create her own fine works. Anne Frank died at a young age, before she could reap the fruits of her diary, but left words that are used by others for inspiration.

Example 5 # Prankster by the Name of I.M. Wrong

While visiting the ancient city of Exeter in southwest England, a man dressed in a top hat, cloak and black suit handed me his card: I.M. Wrong. With that, he threw preserves in my face, and then gave me a swift kick in the pants. After cleaning my face, I found he was gone, and I am wronged.

Two days later, while sitting in the fourth-row balcony of the opera house, a man dressed in a forest green suit and green gloves sat next to me. He was holding a box made of small wooden branches. He opened the side of the box and whistled; inside there were a dozen tiny mice, each at least one hundred times smaller than an ordinary mouse. At his whistle, they jumped on me – my head, face and neck. They did not bite or scratch, but licked my nose, ear, lips, and chin. I felt a wonderful, terrible tickling sensation. I laughed hard and screamed very loud, and disrupted the opera for at least ten minutes. The man whistled again, and the mice jumped back into the box. Before I could stop laughing and gain my composure, he and his miniature mice were gone. I.M. Wrong had wronged me again.

The next afternoon I visited the local market near the town square. Many people were dressed in costumes of various types. An intriguing costume was made with small strips of wood painted black and designed as an intricate building. It was depicted as four stories, with a clock tower and clock. Inside, a man held up the building; his arms were in the eaves, and in the round clock opening appeared the man's face. All costumed people were walking and dancing to the music of a violin and a drum. All were walking and dancing by me. The black wooden house costume was near me, and when it started to spin, the end of the building hit me, and I fell to the cobblestone street. The man inside looked at me, then laughed at me and yelled, "Wrong or not, my name is I.M. Wrong."

The following day I was walking up ancient steps, when, without my knowledge, Mr. Wrong planted two metal stakes on the outside of the steps. After tying one end of the string to the far stake, he held the other end across the steps. Then, as I approached, he tied it to the other stake. Not seeing the string, I caught my right shoe and fell. I.M. Wrong immediately tied me up, and then, after pouring wine and water over me, he was gone. I grabbed my pocketknife, cut myself loose and was after him. I ran, jumped, and tackled the wrong man – yes, he was the Wrong I was after, I.M. Wrong. I am wrong.

I realized I had been wronged by I.M. Wrong, though I was never really hurt physically. Why did he pick me out for his pranks? I must try to get even. Why, there he is, holding twenty-five balloons. I'll knock him down and slap his face.

I run over and push the man down. All twenty-five balloons float skyward. When I look up at him, it's not I.M. Wrong, and yet I.M. Wrong wins again, as I am wrong.

The End

Chapter 12

Diarist Sites

In America and throughout the world, diarists have made literary contributions. They have also made contributions in other fields. Thus governments, individuals and societies have recognized their worth to humanity and have made a place for them, places for people to come to visit: a grave marker, a museum, a house, a fort, a church, a pond (like Walden Pond) or a shrine of some form.

This chapter was written for those who want to visit these shrines, gather information and experience the nostalgia of these special sites. They are few in number compared to all of the landmarks on earth that could be mentioned; the sites I've included here are predominantly those of the major diarists.

1. Ralph Waldo Emerson (1803-1882)

Emerson was a diarist extraordinaire. After writing more than one hundred and fifty volumes over many years, he wanted to find certain ideas, themes and concepts in his diary volumes. It took over five years of indexing to find them. From this research came the first series of essays: History, Self-reliance, Compensation, Spiritual Laws, Love, Friendship, Prudence, Heroism, The Over Soul and Circles. Then came the second series of essays: the Poet, Experience, Character, Intelligence, Art, Manners, Gifts, Nature, Politics and Nominalist and Realist.

He was not only a diarist. He was also a poet, and was considered one of the great American poets of his day.

He earned his living mainly by lecturing and being on a traveling circuit.

In 1829, Emerson visited Europe, meeting Wordsworth and his sister Dorothy Wordsworth (a diarist), Coleridge and Carlyle.

He acquired, from around 1834, one circle of friends (all within the town of Concord, Massachusetts) that came to include Amos Bronson Alcott (Louisa May's father), Margaret Fuller, Henry David Thoreau, James Very and Nathaniel Hawthorne.

It was Emerson's idea that the diary is like a savings bank account. The words, sentences, paragraphs, concepts that are placed in the diary are your deposits. When you go back to read your diary, and take out the deposits – that is your interest.

At the time of his death, he was recognized as the foremost writer and thinker of his country.

List of Sites
* To find Emerson's sites you must go to Concord, Ma., about 18 miles from Boston. His house is now a museum.
* He is buried alongside his family at Writer's Ridge in Sleepy Hollow Cemetery, Concord, Ma.
* Perhaps the best place to find Emerson's writing is the basement of the Concord Public Library where there's a special collection of his works.

2. Henry David Thoreau (1817-1862)

Thoreau was born and raised in Concord, Ma. He graduated from Harvard in 1837 and lived in the home of R.W. Emerson from 1841 to 1843. He was associated with such transcendentalists as Bronson Alcott, George Ripley and Margaret Fuller. He retired to Walden Pond on July 4, 1845, and stayed until September 6, 1847. There he devoted himself to a study of nature and to writing. His journal writing, manuscripts and letters were published in twenty volumes in 1906, titled *The Writings of Henry David Thoreau*.

It is said that he loved nature as a mistress, going to her for better company, and devoting a lifetime to the observation and enjoyment of her ways.

In the basement of J. Pierport Morgan Library in New York City, there's a sturdy wooden box made by Thoreau, which contains thirty-odd ledgers that comprise his famous journals. The journals consist of over two million words. His idea was to use the journals as a source for future books and essays.

Like Emerson, Thoreau is buried in Writer's Ridge, within Sleepy Hollow Cemetery, Concord, next to his family and not far from the Emerson family, the Alcott family and the Hawthorne family.

List of Sites
- Writer's Ridge within Sleepy Hollow Cemetery, Concord, Ma.
- Emerson's House in Concord (where he lived for two years).
- A replica of the cabin at Walden Pond, Concord, Ma. (Walden Pond has been declared a United States Historic Landmark.)

3. Meriwether Lewis (1774-1809) and William Clark (1770-1838)

According to *Webster's Biographical Dictionary*, President Jefferson appointed his private secretary, Meriwether Lewis, to lead an exploration of the Louisiana Purchase and selected William Clark as co-leader. The exploration (1804-06) went up the Missouri River to its source, over the great divide, and descended the Columbia River to the Pacific Ocean. They brought back the flora and fauna of the area and the diaries of several men.

Within the above parameter, much was discovered, history was made and many stories were told.

<u>List of Diary Sites</u>

There are several sites along the Lewis and Clark trail; the four, below, seem to be the most prominent.

- Missouri Historical Society,

  St. Louis, Missouri.

  Museum of exhibits.

- Fort Atkins State Historical Park,

  Omaha, Nebraska.

  Historical Fort – First council with Indians.

- Sacajawea State Park,

  Washington Tri-cities,

  Pasco, Washington.

  Museum.

- Fort Classop Natural Memorial

  Astoria, Oregon.

  Replica Fort, Museum and Bookstore.

  (This site is a National Historic Landmark and run by the National Park Service.)

4. John Muir (1838-1912)

Born in Scotland, John Muir came to America in 1849 at the age of eleven. He kept journals of his travels, including during his stay in Yosemite, as well as other places. He was mainly a naturalist and discovered many Muir trails, which have been named after him. He became friends with presidents Theodore Roosevelt and Howard Taft. He was instrumental in establishing the National Park Service, National Parks and millions of acres to be withheld for the benefit of the public.

List of Sites

- The John Muir National Historical Landmark Site is located in Martinez, California, within the San Francisco Bay Area. His Victorian residence, and part of his first ranch, are preserved by the National Park Service and administered by them. (Muir lived there from 1890 to 1914.) Within the house is his famous "scribble den", where he wrote.
- You can view the web site on the Internet at: www.sierraclub.org/john_muir_exhibit, and click on the button for John Muir National Historic Site.

5. John Adams (1735-1826)

John Adams was the second president of the United States (1797-1801). He nominated George Washington as Commander-in-Chief of the Army at the Continental Congress (1774). He was appointed as envoy to Great Britain (1785). He was elected vice-president of the United States in 1796, and later defeated Jefferson for President. He was one of the signers of the Declaration of Independence.

His diary was published in four volumes (known as "the Adam's papers") by the Belknap Press of Harvard University Press, Cambridge, Ma., in 1962.

The diary has proved to be a quarry of information on the rise of revolutionary resistance in New England, debates in early continental Congress, and diplomacy and financing of the American Revolution. The diary's historical value may well prove secondary to its literary value and human interest.

John Adams was an extraordinary human being, a master of robust, idiomatic language and a superb diarist.

List of Sites
- John Adams' birthplace is administered by the National Park Service and is a National Historic Landmark; the address is 133 Franklin St., Quincy, Ma.
- 141 Franklin St., Quincy, Ma., is the home where his son, John Adam's, was born. Both homes are the property of the city of Quincy and are maintained as museums by the Quincy Historic Society.

6. John Quincy Adams (1767-1848)

John Quincy Adams was the sixth president of the United States and the son of John Adams. He was elected to the U.S. Senate, was appointed to the U.S. Supreme Court in 1811 (but declined), then became a Representative in Congress. One of the negotiators of peace after the War of 1812, he was also Minister to Great Britain.

He kept meticulous records in his diary for fifty-one years (from 1794 to 1845), which consisted of penetrating insights, opinions and personal doubts. (His diary is one of the most valuable in American history.) He walked with Czar Alexander I, had an audience with George III, dined with Wellington and saw Napoleon return to Paris.

Here's a quote about Adams from *The World's Great Diaries*, edited by Philip Dunaway and Mel Evans: "A frosty, irascible little man with a high shrill voice and a biting pen spent an hour or more a day from youth to old age keeping a remarkable record of his own life and lives of those around him." His diary is such an extraordinary document that had he done nothing else he would still be remembered.

List of Sites
- For his diary sites, see those listed for his father, John Adams.

7. Mary Boykin Chesnut (1823-1886)

Mary Chesnut recorded the events of the American Civil War. Her work is considered to be the best diary of that period.

Her diary was published in 1904, eighteen years after her demise. Ninety-six years after her death, in 1982, she was awarded the Pulitzer Prize for History.

List of Sites
- On March 15, 2000, Mary's home in Camden, South Carolina, became a new National Historic Landmark, and is overseen by the National Park Service. (Designation of landmark status is the federal government's official recognition of the national importance of historic properties.)

8. Nathaniel Hawthorne (1804-1864)

Hawthorne's published diaries are entitled: *American Notebooks, English Notebooks, French Notebooks and Italian Notebooks.* Here is a sample entry: "Sept 1, 1842 – Mr. Thoreau dined with us yesterday...He is keen and delicate observer of nature – a genuine observer of nature."

Hawthorne is famous for his novels *Twice Told Tales* (1846), *Mosses from the Old Manse* (1846), *The Scarlet Letter* (1850), *The House of Seven Gables* (1851) and others works.

List of Sites
- Hawthorne lived in Old Manse, Concord, Ma., from 1842-1846. This was the home of W.M. Emerson (built in 1770), Ralph Waldo's father, where Waldo witnessed Salvos of the revolution.

- U.S. Custom's House, Salem, Ma. He worked there as a surveyor from 1847-1849. He describes the musty and cobwebbed second floor, where he discovered the records that inspired the novel, *The Scarlet Letter*.
- The House of Seven Gables, 54 Turner Street, Salem, Ma. This is the house where Nathaniel Hawthorne was born. One of his famous novels is titled *The House of Seven Gables*. The house has been restored for the public.

9. Oliver Wendall Holmes Jr. (1814-1935)

Oliver Wendall Holmes Jr. was the son of Oliver Wendall Holmes Sr., the famous physician, essayist and poet who wrote *Old Iron Sides*. He was a first lieutenant in the 20th Regiment of the Massachusetts Volunteers and he saw action at Balls Bluff during the Civil War. He was wounded there, then again at Antietam and Chancellorville. The first time he was shot through the chest, another time through the neck (yet he survived and came back to fight again). His father was a close friend of Ralph Waldo Emerson. Holmes Jr. came to Emerson at the end of the Civil War for personal advice about his future.

Holmes published his wartime journal, titled *Touched with Fire: Civil War Letters and Diaries of Oliver Wendell Holmes, Jr.* Following his interest in law, he became the Presiding Judge of the United States Supreme Court. Holmes took pride in his wartime regiment, and in his accomplishments as a lawyer and judge. In an 1884 speech, he used the phrase "in our youth our hearts were touched by fire." The speech also contained a tribute to the fallen men of the 20th Regiment of Massachusetts.

List of Sites
- Holmes' gravesite is at Arlington National Cemetery.

10. Louisa May Alcott (1832-1888)

Alcott's neighbors in Concord, Ma., were her father's friends Ralph Waldo Emerson, Margaret Fuller, Nathaniel Hawthorne and Henry David Thoreau. They (and her father) all wrote diaries.

Louisa began her journal at age ten, and continued it until a few days before her death. At age ten she wrote, "I rose at five and had my bath. I love cold water." When she wrote *Little Women,* she needed to look no further than her journals, as the story was there.

List of Sites
- The Wayside House, 455 Lexington Road, Concord, Ma., (also called the Hillside House). In 1845, Louisa's grandfather died and left the Alcotts $1000. Mr. Emerson added $500 to that amount, and the Alcotts bought this farmhouse. At last, Louisa had her own room (she recalled that this house and period of time was the happiest of her childhood).
- Orchard House, 399 Lexington Road, Concord, Ma. In 1858, thirteen years after living in Hillside House, the Alcotts moved. The twelve-room house was painted and papered by the Alcott girls. Here in her second story bedroom (and writing study), Louisa wrote *Little Women.*
- Burial site at Writer's Ridge within Sleepy Hollow Cemetery, Concord, Ma., within the family plot.

11. Herman Melville (1819-1891)

"Melville is known today for his famous novel *Moby Dick* and other works. He kept a diary and especially one detailing a voyage from New York to London. From October 11th, 1849, to November 14th, 1849, he takes the reader aboard with him. He describes fellow passengers, his grand stateroom, the seasickness aboard, playing cards and shuffleboard. Yet, all in good flow of language." (This quote is from *The Journal of a Visit to London and the Continent* by Herman Melville, 1849, edited by Eleanor Melville Metcalf.)

With twenty-four days at sea, during calm and stormy weather, and with no duties, Melville had plenty of time to write. He pondered the past and the future. Being a sailor, he knew all about the ship he was on.

List of Sites
- Herman Melville's "Arrowhead" is a registered National Historic Landmark. It was Melville's home from 1850 to 1862. It was at Arrowhead that Melville wrote his most famous work, *Moby Dick*, as well as three other novels. Arrowhead is now a museum. It is owned and operated by the Berkshire County Historical Society.

    Arrowhead,

    780 Holmes Road,

    Pittsfield, Ma.

    Telephone: (413) 442-1793.

12. Will Rogers (1879-1935)

In their book *Diary of America*, Josef and Dorothy Berger wrote, "Will Rogers was known for his humor 'and his had a bite.' His gibes at congress were devastating. But the people loved him. At the height of his career, his box office attraction was greater than that of any other entertainer in America." They also quoted him as saying: "I am the only known child in history who claims Nov. 4th as my Birthday, that is election day. Women couldn't vote in those days so my Mother thought she would do something, so she stayed home and gave birth to me. The men were all away. I decided to get even with the government. That's why I have always had it in for politicians."

List of Sites

- Dog Iron Ranch (Will Rogers' birthplace), Oologah, Oklahoma.
- Will Rogers Memorial Museum,

    1720 W Will Rogers Blvd

    Claremore, Oklahoma.

    Will Rogers Memorial Museum is a twenty-acre hilltop in Clarence, Oklahoma. He planned to build a home there, but it was later used for his burial site, in 1944. There is a larger than life statue of him by Jo Davidson; carved on the base are Rogers' infamous words, "I never met a man I didn't like."

- Alaska Memorial.

    The Alaska Memorial is at Point Barrow. In 1944, Will Rogers and Wiley Post were flying alone (their destination was Siberia). They were over the coastline of the Arctic Sea and Point Barrow, Alaska when they crashed into the ocean within a few hundred feet of shore. This memorial is a rounded building with a bronze plaque, memorializing Rogers and Post.

13. Mark Twain (1835-1910)

Twain kept diaries and notebooks for nearly fifty years.

From his notebook, prepared for publication by Albert Paine in 1935, comes the story of his sailing trip from San Francisco to New York City. The story includes a vast storm at sea, cholera aboard with eight people who died buried below the water with weights to hold them down (and fear that anyone could be next to catch the deadly disease).

- The Mark Twain House: a nineteen-room, Tiffany-decorated mansion where he wrote *The Adventures of Tom Sawyer*, *Huckleberry Finn* and *A Connecticut Yankee in King Arthur's Court*.

  The Mark Twain house is located at:

  > 351 Farmington Avenue
  >
  > Hartford, Connecticut 06105.

14. Father Junipero Serra (1713-1784)

Serra was a Spanish missionary in America, and he was one of the most important missionaries in the new world. He was born in Majorca in 1713, and joined the Franciscan order at the age of sixteen. He went to Mexico City in 1750 to start a new life.

The diary of Father Serra concerns the expedition from Loreto to San Diego. He established the site of the San Diego Mission in 1769 (the first of eight missions).

During his trek, he recorded his experience of seeing a valley full of rose bushes so thick that he couldn't enter the valley. He also recorded his feelings when holding Indian babies.

List of Sites
- Burial place:

  > Carmel Mission,
  >
  > Carmel, Ca.

  A statue, *Sacafacus*, by Joe Mora is there (and another statue in the courtyard).

- A statue:

     San Fernando Mission

     San Fernando, Ca.

     (A statue of him standing next to an Indian boy.)
- A bronze statue by Ettore Cadorin was donated by the State of California to the National Statuary Hall Collection, Washington D.C.

15. Opal Whiteley (1897-1992)

Whiteley was probably the most noted child diarist of all time. It is believed that she was born in France to French parents. She arrived in Oregon after both her parents died. She wrote of them as "Angel Mother" and "Angel Father." She lived with foster parents, the Whiteleys, in a lumber camp near Cottage Grove, Oregon. Every chance she got she'd venture out into the woods. When she returned home she had recorded (on a scrap of paper) what she saw, heard and felt while in the woods.

In 1919, at the office of Ellery Sedgwick of the Atlantic Monthly (in Boston, Ma.), Opal presented a manuscript of a book she had written. The editor Sedgwick didn't like it, yet was intrigued by this young woman. He asked her if she wrote anything else. She admitted she had a diary, but on slips of paper, and these were torn up by a foster sister. They were in a box in Los Angeles. The box was brought to Boston. Sedgwick's mother and Opal pieced them together like a jigsaw puzzle.

In 1920, Opal's diary, *The Journal of an Understanding Heart*, was published serially for six months in the Atlantic Monthly, and then into a hardback version.

There are one hundred and two characters in the book. Her favorites were Brave Horatius (the collie dog), Thomas Chatterton Jupiter Zeus (a wonderful wood rat) and Lucian Horace Avid Virgil (a toad), to name a few.

List of Sites
- A trail near Cottage Grove, Oregon, known as "Opal's Fairyland."

16. General Gaspar de Portola (1723-1784)

Portola was a Spanish soldier in America. He was appointed Governor of California in 1767. With Spanish soldiers and missionaries (including Father Junipero Serra) he made the thousand mile march from Velicata in Baja California to Monterey in Alta California. He founded San Diego and Monterey in 1769.

During this march, Portola kept a diary. It's known as the official account of the Portola Expedition of 1769 and 1770.

List of Sites
California:
- In San Diego, California, there's a plaque and wall sculpture at Punta de los Muertos, San Diego.
- In Monterrey, California, there's a plaque where the Presidio and settlements were founded. At the Civic Center, a square is named Portola Plaza and there stands a statue of Portola.
- In San Francisco, California, there's a mural in the Episcopalian Grace Church showing Portola, Serra and Spanish soldiers.

Spain:
- In Barcelona there's a statue of Portola and a metal plate, "sue Bicentaria, 1786-1986".

- In Lerida, there's a bronze group of sculptures of Portola, Serra, Lt. Foges and soldiers.
- In Balogues, there's a statue and plaque commemorating Portola.

17. Richard Henry Dana (1815-1882)

Dana was a sailor, author and lawyer. He sailed from Boston around the Cape Horn to California (1834-1836).

His diary was published in 1968 (published by the Belnap Press of Harvard Press, Cambridge, Ma.) It's in three volumes. The diary includes his voyage at sea, the time he was a lawyer and comments about his social circle. His journal is formidable in magnitude, running to six hundred thousand words.

Using the details about his voyage that he recorded in his diary, he published his adventures (in 1840) under the title *Two Years Before the Mast*. It became a worldwide bestseller.

On January 29, 1842, he wrote: "Dined with Charles Dickens – like him very much. He is perfectly natural and unpretending." Dickens was asked if there were any magistrates in London as Fang in Oliver Twist. He said, "One just such and many more like him."

Dana was a member of the famous Saturday Club that met monthly in Boston. On December 16, 1854, he wrote: "Dined in select company of Emerson, Lowell, Alcott"... (and others). "It was very agreeable. Emerson is a excellent dinner table man, always a gentleman, never bores or preaches or dictates... So, indeed, has Alcott and it is quite surprising to see the transcendentalists appearing well as men of the world."

On August 6, 1857, he wrote again about the Saturday Club. He wrote that the club was very important, and noted that the other members were Longfellow, Agassiz, Judge Hoar, Holmes Sr., Ward, Woodman and himself.

In 1835, he wrote about a special shore in Southern California (Orange County) now known as Dana Point.

List of Sites
- Replica of the ship called Pilgrim at Dana Point, California.

18. Walt Whitman (1819-1892)

Walt Whitman is famous for his book *Leaves of Grass*. Whitman's notebooks are at the Library of Congress's American Memory Collection. These four notebooks were lost in 1942, and then re-surfaced in 1995. They contain some early fragments of *Leaves of Grass*.

List of Sites
- Known as "Whitmanland," this site includes his birthplace (246 Old Whitman Road), which was restored by the State of New York. Other Whitman residences in West Hills are also there, in South Huntington and Long Island, New York. It is now a State Historic Site. There are over five hundred acres of "Whitmanland." There is also the Joseph Whitman House and the Whitman-Carll House.

19. Christopher Columbus (1451-1506)

The following paragraph about Columbus is from *Webster's Biographical Dictionary*:
"Discoverer of America. Born near or at Genoa, Italy. Went to sea at an early age. Settled in Lisbon, Portugal (c. 1477) married and had a son, Diego. He

believed the earth was round, and conceived the idea of reaching Asia by sailing due west. Ferdinand and Isabella agreed to an expedition. Sailed from Palos (August 3, 1492) and sited land (October 12, 1492) at one of the Bahamas. Continued and sailed north coast of Cuba, and Haiti. On his second voyage with seventeen ships and one thousand five hundred men, discovered Dominica, then sailed westward and discovered Jamaica. On his third voyage discovered Trinidad and probably discovered Honduras and Panama."

The diary of Columbus is the only day-to-day account of the discovery of America. He gave his diary to Ferdinand and Isabella (which ended up in the royal archives, where it was copied). Later, originals (as well as some copies) were lost. Finding a copy, a grandson translated it into Italian in 1571.

<u>List of Sites</u>
- The greatest site the United States has ever had was The World's Columbian Exposition in Chicago in 1893-94. It was in commemoration of the 400th Anniversary of the discovery of America. It was immense in size and impressive to the millions of people who attended. The only building remaining is the Palace of Fine Arts (now Chicago's Museum of Science and Industry). The best place to view the building, grounds and the rest of the Exposition is on the Internet: World's Columbian Exposition (also see its links).
- The Columbian theater, museum and Art Center, Wamego, Kansas. Mural paintings 11 feet by 16 feet in size and other artifacts from the World's Columbian Exposition are here. Wamego is thirteen miles from Manhattan, Kansas.
- The monument to Columbus in New York's Central Park.

20. Samuel Pepys, Esquire (1633-1703)

Dunaway and Evans, in A *Treasury of The Worlds Great Diaries*, wrote: "Out of more than 2000 pages of what is undoubtedly the most remarkable diary ever written there steps a man. Short, plump, bewigged and powdered, he advances in mincing steps with his gold-headed cane in hand, his thick sensual lips slightly parted. He stops and turns upon the reader his warm, disarming smile. This is Samuel Pepys."

List of Sites
- Pepys is best found at his library (The Pepys Library) at Magdalane College, Cambridge University, England.

It's an enjoyable trip from London to Cambridge, and by rail it's only one hour. Make sure, first, that the college is open. (During summer vacation the college and library are closed.)

It's best to write a letter to the librarian (or send an e-mail), noting that you want to visit (also give him the date). He will undoubtedly write back that all will go well. He'll have your letter when you arrive and someone will probably escort you around. You may also just go in and make your own tour.

What will you see there? First, Cambridge is a wonderful town; together with the university grounds it looks like a fairy wonderland (or a Disneyland put together in the 14th and 15th centuries with no façade). You'll also see the Cam River, people in long boats (punting), and its bridge (hence the name of the city and University.)

Within the Pepys library, there's the fascination of the three thousand leather bound volumes that Pepys gave to his college (they're still being used by the University students). In cases under glass is one of his manuscript diaries.

It's open so you can see the page, but because it's written in his *own code,* it's undecipherable to the unknowledgeable. In the same case is a small shirt pocket book measuring three inches by four inches, which was Sir Francis Drake's nautical almanac of 1546. It is said that Drake carried this book in his shirt pocket when he circumnavigated the world. Over a hundred years later Pepys borrowed the book (when he was head of the admiralty), and never returned it.

Because the diary was written in his own code, it is assumed he could write freely without fear of anyone reading it. Not his wife, friends, servants, or even the King, were able to read it.

21. Francis Kilvert (1840-1879)

Kilvert's diary gives a picture of 19th Century country life in central Wales and Radnorshire. A young minister with the temperament of a poet – a man who loved life and his fellow man.

"*Monday, 26 December*
Much warmer and almost thaw. Left Clyro at 11am.
At Chippenham my father and John were on the platform. After dinner we opened a hamper of game sent by the Venables, and found in it a pheasant, a hare, a brace of rabbits, a brace of woodcocks, and a turkey."
(This is an extract from Kilvert's Diary, volume one, between the years 1870-1879, edited by William Plomer.)

Mr. E.J.C. West, secretary to the Kilvert Society, explained: "There are about seven hundred members in our society and many of them the descendants of those persons written about by the reverend in the diary." Mr. West was proud to be called "the dog's body," as he had so many jobs to do within the society.

Ardizzone's Kilvert is a book for younger readers. It contains selections from the diary and hand drawings.

Reverend Kilvert was compared favorably with Dorothy Wordsworth, and in some respects, to Samuel Pepys.

List of Sites
- There are many sites in Clyro and Chippenham districts; it's best to contact the Kilvert Society in Ross-on-Wye, Hereford, Hay-on-Wye, or Clyro, all in England.

22. Virginia Woolf (1882-1941)

In 1957, Leonard Woolf, widower of Virginia, made an arrangement with the Berg Collection that the 27 manuscript diaries of Virginia would be their property after his death. The Berg Collection is within the Public Library of the city of New York.

Virginia usually wrote her diary after tea. It was written indiscreetly and is filled with amazing family gossip and unsparing portraits of friends.

List of Sites
- A farmhouse, known as the Asheham House, in East Sussex, England. This was Leonard and Virginia's home after their London home was destroyed in WWII.

23. Frida Kahlo (1907-1954)

Kahlo's diary was kept from 1944 to 1954. It contains her thoughts, poems and dreams. It also contains reflections about her stormy relationship with her husband, Diego Rivera, Mexico's most famous artist.

The diary was published in 1995 and consists of entries in her handwriting as well as drawings using many colors. Thus, the book is her art in every way.

The diary also contains caricatures, designs, animals, pictures, self-portraits, all surrounded by her handwriting. It's a magnificent work. The second half of the published book is in English with printed words and paintings in black and white.

Frida was a professional painter. By 1944, she had produced about one hundred paintings. In 1938, she sold four paintings to the motion picture actor Edward G. Robinson.

List of Sites

- The Frida Kahlo Museum, Casa Azul, 247 Londres, at Allende in Cyoacan, Mexico City. This is where Frida was born, grew up and later lived with Diego Rivera from 1941 until her death at age 47 in 1954.

24. Anne Frank (1929-1945)

Anne Frank (Amelia Marie) was born in Frankfurt, Germany, on December 6 1929, and died in March of 1945.

On the 12th of June, 1942, she wrote, "I hope I shall be able to confide in you completely, as I have never been able to do in anyone before, and I hope that you will be a great support and comfort to me." (Anne Frank: *The Dairy of a Young Girl*, copyright 1952 by Otto H Frank.)

Mrs. Eleanor Roosevelt, wife to President Franklin D. Roosevelt, said of Anne Frank, "the young are not afraid of telling the truth."

Anne Frank wrote to "Kitty" (the name she gave her diary) from June 1942 to August 1944. On August 4, 1944, the police raided the "secret annex," where her family was hiding. An informer had revealed the existence of the secret annex. All eight members living there were seized. Anne and her sister, Margot, died of typhus at the Concentration camp Bergen-Belsen in March 1945.

Anne's diary is among the most enduring documents of the twentieth century. Since publication in 1947, it has been read by tens of millions of people all over the world.

List of Sites

- Secret Annex, Amsterdam, the Netherlands.
- The Anne Frank Center USA

    584 Broadway, Suite 408

    New York, New York 10012

    USA.

    The Exhibition and Education Center, founded in 1993, sponsors exhibitions, lectures and special events that commemorate the life of Anne Frank.

25. Dorothy Wordsworth (1771-1855)

Dorothy Wordsworth began her journals in 1798, and they were published in 1889, 1897 and 1904. She describes the domestic country life at Alfoxen and Grasmere; she also wrote her accounts of Scotland and the European Continent.

She and her famous brother, William Wordsworth, as well as Samuel Taylor Coleridge, lived together in Dove Cottage in the Lake District, England.

No portrait of Dorothy exists except one, taken in old age. But De Quincy gives us his impression of her in youth; he writes, "Gypsy tan, from constant exposure to sun and wind," and of her eyes he writes, "not soft nor bold: but they were wild and startling."

On the 7th of March 1798, she wrote in her journal: "One only leaf upon the top of a tree – the sole remaining leaf – danced round and round like a rag blown by the wind."

She writes of longing for her brother, William, when he's away. She walks for miles to get mail from him, and waits along the road and wood where he may be coming home.

She climbs the hills at Grasmere, picking flowers and then transplanting them into her own garden at Dove Cottage.

Dorothy Wordsworth's diary writing has been compared to the writings of Francis Kilvert. Both wrote about nature. Both wrote about their love of others (good descriptive writing). They knew one another, had met, but didn't have enough time to establish a friendship.

In the *Illustrated Lakeland Journals*, there's a portrait of Dorothy at age sixty-two (in color), a sketch of Dove Cottage in the early nineteenth century, a sketch of Dorothy sitting in an ancient wheelchair in her early seventies, and other sketches (as well as a map of Grasmere in 1800). For Dorothy Wordsworth fans, this book is a must: *Dorothy Wordsworth Illustrated Lakeland Journals* by Diamond Books, a division of Harper Collins, reprinted in 1992.

<u>List of Sites</u>
- Dove Cottage and Wordsworth Museum, Town End, Grasmere Ambleside, Cumbria, England (in the Lake District). (The Wordsworth Museum has Dorothy's journals, and William's and Coleridge's writings.)

26. Pet Marjory Fleming (1803-1811)

There is a statue of Marjory Fleming, seated, on her grave at the cemetery in Kirkcaldy, Scotland. She looks straight ahead. There's a pen in her right hand and diary book in her lap. Her dress comes down to her shoes. On the gravestone, beneath her, is carved: "Marjory Fleming 'Pet Marjory' died at Kirkcaldy, December 19th, 1811 aged 8 years and 11 months. The youngest immortal in the world of letters."

It's noted by Alexandra Johnson (in her book *The Hidden Writer: Diaries and the Creative Life*) that the nickname "Pet" was never used in Marjory's lifetime. Two men, Brougham Farnie and Dr. John Brown, recognizing Marjory's talent for writing at an early age, wrote and published stories about her. They added the nickname "Pet" to her name. The gravestone has the name "Pet Marjory" and was probably carved after the stories were written, and it was believed to be her true name.

List of Sites

* To see Marjory's statue, go to Edinburgh, and then take the train to St. Andrews. Over a red bridge and over the Firth of Forth, get off at Kirkcaldy (about 20 miles). Take a cab or other transportation to the cemetery.
* There's also a museum in the town, and behind glass cases are several of her personal items.

Marjory wrote poetry within her journal. Here are two of these:

Three Turkeys (Dedicated to Mrs. H. Crawford)

Three turkeys fair their last have breathed,
And now this world for ever leaved;

Their father and their mother too,

They sigh and weep as well as you;

Indeed, the rats their bones have crunched,

Into eternity theire laanched.

A direful death indeed they had,

As wad put any parent mad;

But she was more than usual calm,

She did not give a single dam.

Mary Queen of Scots

Queen Mary was much loved by all,

Both by the great and by the small,

But hark! her soul to heaven doth rise!

And I suppose she has gained a prize–

For I do think she would not go

Into the *awful* place below;

There is a thing that I must tell,

Elizabeth went to fire and hell;

He who would teach her to be civil,

It must be her great friend the divil!

(These are from John Brown M.D.'s book titled: *Pet Marjory: A Story of a Child Life Fifty Years Ago.* It is published by T.N. Foulis, 1905.)

Chapter 13

Published Diary Books

Introduction

This chapter provides lists, commentary and examples of a variety of diary books. All diary books have something educational to offer, whether it be history, writing styles or ideas about writing.

There are as many diary writing styles as there are diarists. Yet, the goal for all diarists is that they express themselves the best way they can, in a way that is most natural to them.

We can learn from the diaries of others, when we're inspired by their writing style. For example, Mr. Pepys' style is distinct, and includes details about the transportation he used to get where he was going. He wrote that – he took a carriage, he walked, he took a boat down the Thames.

Henry David Thoreau is another example of a diarist with a distinct style. It is well known that he spent his days thinking, pondering and considering what was important to him. The day being over, he wrote these thoughts in his diary. Thus, his thinking was preparation for his diary writing.

Anaïs Nin said that she *had* to write, "While the seeds were bursting." She wrote at various times of the day; her writing was fresh and included details about her experiences, observations and her thoughts. She had arguments with her friend Henry Miller about the "seeds"; in contrast to Nin's spontaneity, Miller had to sleep on his thoughts before he could write.

This chapter covers information about diary books in the following categories:

- Diary Book Lists
- Instructional Diary Books
- Anthologies
- Commentaries
- Narratives
- Illustrated Diaries
- Children's Diaries

Diary Book Lists

1. American Diaries

American Diaries is a book of annotated diaries written prior to 1861. This work was compiled by William Matthews, and published by J.S. Canner Company, copyright 1959.

Mr. Matthews begins this book with a narrative about Reverend Francis Higginson, whose 1629 sea diary captured the voyage from England to New England.

Matthews then moves on to discuss the 1630 journal by John Winthrop (Governor of Boston), a historical journal known as his *History of New England*; the diary is an impersonal daily record of public events.

The last entry mentioned in the book is that of Lester Frank Ward, a sociologist and geologist. His private diary is intimate and delightful, written by an eager, intelligent Victorian.

2. American Diaries in Manuscript.

American Diaries in Manuscript is a descriptive bibliography of diaries that were written between 1580 and 1954. This book was compiled by William Matthews, and was published by University of Georgia Press. Most of the manuscript diaries listed in this book were never published. Each listing includes the name of the writer, the time span of the diary and a summary of the contents of the diary as well as where it's located.

3. American Diaries

American Diaries is an annotated bibliography of published American diaries and journals by Laura Arskey, Nancy Pries and Marcia Reed (published by Gale Research Company, Detroit, copyright 1983). It is an extension and revision of the work by William Matthews, *American Diaries*. It contains similar annotation to William Matthews' book.

These two volumes extend Matthews' time period to include the Civil War and up to the year 1980. In addition, they include diaries excluded by Matthews, such as the Spanish explorers' (Gaspar de Portola and Father Junipero Serra).

4. British Diaries 1442-1942

British Diaries, An Annotated Bibliography of British Diaries Written between 1442 and 1942 was compiled by William Matthews and published by The Regents of the University of California, copyright 1950.

An example from the book: "1837 De Rothschild, Lady Louisa (1821-1910), Philanthropist, Social diarist, July, 1837 to January 1878 (extracts); quiet details of family life in London; her reading; Court life and society; Victoria and Albert; musical evenings and musicians; visits to Italy; Jewish Life; sport and family life; a valuable record."

Instructional Diary Books

1. At a Journal Workshop

At a Journal Workshop by Ira Progoff was published by Dialogue House Library, copyright 1975. In the years following publication, classes at major universities in the U.S. taught the course known as the Intensive Journal. The course was based upon Progoff's book.

This is basically a psychological workbook, including instructions on how to use Progoff's system.

In his book, Progoff teaches many techniques. Some of his subjects include *Journal Feedback*, the *Period Log* and the *Daily Log*. However, his major concepts are those concerning *Dialogue*. Dialogues enable one to converse (in writing) with other persons and with our bodies ("We make contact with the world of nature, with music, physical act of dance and sports, sexuality..."). One can also have dialogues with dreams, society and inner wisdom.

This book is an outstanding work. It's deep and complex; hence, it may be best to learn the precepts in a class where the teacher knows all aspects of Progoff's theories and how to use the exercises.

2. The New Diary.

The New Diary was written by Tristain Rainer and includes a preface by Anaïs Nin. It was published by Tarcher Inc., copyright 1978. This is a sound book for the diary writer. Rainer covers many aspects of diary writing and she follows the precepts of Jung, Nin, Progoff and Milner. Then she offers many diary techniques.

3. One to One: Self-understanding through Journal Writing

One to One: Self-understanding through Journal Writing was written by Christine Baldwin and published by Mr. Evans and Company, copyright 1977. Baldwin shows how the journal can have a relationship to our minds, to a thought and to a friend.

4. The Creative Journal, The Art of Finding Yourself.

The Creative Journal, The Art of Finding Yourself was written by Lucia Capacchione and published by Swallow Press, copyright 1979. When ill and in pain and confusion, she encourages the use of writing and drawing in the diary.

5. American Diary Literature 1620-1799

American Diary Literature 1620-1799 was written by Steven E Kagle and published by Twayne Publications, copyright 1979. This is a book on historical diaries of the colonial period and the few years following the American Revolution. Professor Kagle finds beauty of form and emotional effect in the many diaries he examines in this book. In the first chapter, Kagle writes about the diary as art. He states that to be artistic in a diary one doesn't write facts as a journalist would, but words are colored by the individual's sensibility. He quotes Gide, "Rather than recounting his life as he has lived it, he (the artist) must live it as he will recount it." He promotes the idea that the diary must be an *ideal portrait of life*.

Kagle also discusses the religious journals of the Puritans, Quakers and the Methodists.

In the travel chapter, he examines Alexander Hamilton's diary and, particularly, the manners between Hamilton and those of the non-educated class. Then in the same chapter he cites Philip Vickers Fithier's statements of the difference between Virginia and his native state New Jersey; Fithier was initiated to the existence slavery on the plantation where he taught in Virginia, where as there were none in New Jersey.

The book – the commentary and the various quotations referred to– is written with a sound knowledge of history.

For the serious dairy writer, this book is one of the finest you will find.

Anthologies (Compilations)

1. Small Voices

Small Voices by Josef and Dorothy Berger was published by Paul S. Ericksson, Inc., copyright 1966. The book contains excerpts from many children's diaries, including the diaries of Anaïs Nin (age 11), Opal Whiteley (age 6), Theodore Roosevelt (age 10), Marjory Fleming (age 6) and many others. This is a superior book, one-of-a-kind.

2. The Book of American Diaries

The Book of American Diaries was edited by Randall M. Miller and Linda Patterson Miller and was published by Avon Books, copyright 1995. This book of excerpts includes one entry for each day of the year from various diaries. For example, for January 1, Ebenezer Packman's entry (1726) is included, then Meriwether Lewis' entry from the Oregon Coast (1806). In back of the book is the Dramatis Personal: a list of each diarist's name, date of birth and death, occupation and a short statement about the diarist.

3. Diary of America

Diary of America was edited by Josef and Dorothy Berger, copyright 1957. The first section of the book includes extracts of diaries from 1492 to 1777, entitled "The New World"; Christopher Columbus, William Bradford, Sara Kemble Knight, Alexander Hamilton and Philip Vickers Fithier are in this group. Then the book goes up to 1951 and many great Americans appear in each section. This is a monumental work.

4. Our Private Lives: Journals, Notebooks and Diaries

Our Private Lives: Journals, Notebooks and Diaries was edited by Daniel Halpern, copyright 1988. The first chapter in this book is an essay about diaries by Gail Goodwin. Speaking off-the-cuff, she writes about Kafka and her mother's diary (which was kept at the time she was conceived). She states that she needs to write a diary just as she needs to write fiction. Fiction keeps her organized and diary writing keeps her mind fresh and open. Then she lets us know about codes, mirror writing, mixtures of foreign languages. She has a lot to say in nine pages.

Other writings in the book include Rich Bass's *An Oilman's Notebook*; which is intriguing. Then there is Annie Dillard's notebook; she quotes many writers: "Poe argued that a poem's excitement can last half an hour 'at the most'." – H. Rosenberg. Then Robert Frost: "I met a pacifist who exalted cowardice as the only real hope of ending war."

The book contains excerpts from forty-two writers in all.

5. A Treasury of the World's Great Diaries

A Treasury of the World's Great Diaries was edited by Philip Dunaway and Mel Evans, published by Doubleday and Company, Inc., copyright 1957. This book has been mentioned before on page 22; it is a masterly work.

6. Darkness and Light: Private Writing as Art

Darkness and Light: Private Writing as Art is an anthology of contemporary journals, diaries and notebooks edited by Olivia Dresher and Victor Munoz, copyright 2000. The purpose of the collection is to promote the notion of journals, diaries and notebooks as a valid literary genre.

When looking for contributions the editors stated: "We seek contributors whose inner life is already so rich that it spills out into their journals from a sense of urgency, not as a project or duty.... We are interested in literary, poetic, philosophical, and/or psychological writing which reflects a commitment to the journal as a distinct art form." The editors hoped to discover "those who valued their journals as their life's work," and they "leaned towards accepting serious and introspective writing." (And select they did; they've put together a very worthwhile collection.)

Examples of some of the contributions in the book:

Gleanings (From the Journals, 1964-1989) by Audrey Borenstein

"What if the world you're building within yourself counts the most? What you leave on this earth matters, yes. But it may be that the inner palace and its walled gardens are another reality we haven't even dreamed of as our keep hereafter.

"It seems the more one understands, the more silent one becomes. I want to fling myself before God and say, 'Take everything, everything from me, only watch over them, protect them'. This is, of course, the price the older parent must pay: the awareness of all that lives inside people and of all that might befall one and one's most beloved children.

"Perhaps life is theatre, I suggest to V. The dead and the unborn, all spirits are in the wings...and take possession of us now and again, flying in and flying out. Life is so long, Journal. The radiance is sometimes so intense. And then it leaves as it came – in an instant."

Fragments and Aphorisms: From Notebooks, 1988-1990 by Olivia Dresher

"Almost everything I write in my notebooks begins as a chant in my head. The chant builds and grows; I can't contain it. It must come out as words on paper – to bring the disparity between myself and the world into a less disturbing focus. By defining (or "insighting") what I feel and perceive, the words on the page take on a new dimension: they transcend my own individual life and become art."

"The smell of memories.
Daily memories, always fresh.
Memories as hallucinations,
flashbacks more real than now.
A constant hum that can become
a madness or a sweet companion."

"No passion or truth in niceness.
Adults, politely, lower their eyes,
but the screaming child on the bus today
looked into me for a long time.
I looked back, and thought:
finally, a real face."

"A shadow of a spider on the wall.
The spider radiates self-confidence
to the extreme.
Its purity feels evil.
Its web is an extension of its certainty:
it traps exactly what it needs."

"I am touched by words,
the way I'm touched by the right touch.
To not speak to me is to not touch me.
The celibacy of silence."

7. A Women's Diaries Miscellany

A Women's Diaries Miscellany, edited by Jane Dupree Begos, was published by Magic Circle Press, copyright 1989. It contains essays on women's diaries, including English women's diaries and their history. An article on Quaker diaries is also included, as well as information about the diaries of famous American women. More essays include the topic of women's education in the 19th Century, and the diaries of women who died young. Each essay was written by a different writer.

8. Men Without Masks

Men Without Masks was edited by Michael Rubin, and published by Addison Wesley Publishing Co., copyright 1980. This book is filled with sections of diaries written by different men (including editor Michael Rubin) who had the courage to confront their emotions in order to become more whole themselves.

Which men wear the masks? Those who do not take risks in confronting feelings, since the bravery of self-exploration would be painful. These are the men who are "manly," who bust their heads in football games and isolate themselves in a polar winter. These men do not show their emotions. As boys, they are taught early on to dampen certain feelings and deny other feelings, certainly to control them. They are told to use their intellect and let emotion take a back seat. As men, they use analysis, objectivity and the rigors of logical thinking – areas where feelings are not involved.

Rubin selected the diarists who broke this male stereotype and "had used their hearts as much as their heads as they wrote about their daily lives. I also wanted examples of men still close to the events they describe."

In Michael Rubin's diary, which he wrote while in intensive therapy, he explores his relationship with his mother: "Then I began to realize – no to feel – that everything, all those childhood fears of mine were the result of not having enough of her. I begged for more attention, more love, screamed with rage when I couldn't get it... All the crying I'd done during childhood, in adolescence or into my twenties and even after her death..."

In Alfred Hassler's diary, we find him in prison as a conscientious objector during W W II. He writes: "Last night some wild geese passed overhead flying low, I caught a glimpse of the "V" of their flight. At the very moment of their passage, I could hear the deep, almost silent sobs of one of my fellow convicts. It is no longer a novel sound, but it wrenches my whole spirit with wretchedness whenever I hear it. During the day, the men maintain the cloak of bravado in which they wrap their self-respect; at night, alone in the darkness, their grief and fright sometimes became too much for them to bear."

This book reveals the emotional power of diary writing. Rubin shows the reader how, by expressing themselves, the men who kept diaries were able to better understand themselves and become more human.

Commentaries

1. A Review of English Diaries From the XVIth to the XXth Century

A Review of English Diaries From the XVIth to the XXth Century was compiled and edited by Arthur Ponsonby, Member of Parliament, and published by Butler and Tanner Ltd, London, copyright 1922.

This is a valuable book. Ponsonby's 45-page introduction is an education in itself.

The author begins with a discussion of each diary by offering a bibliographical sketch. Then he includes excerpts and commentary. (His commentaries outweigh the excerpts.)

For Fanney Burney (Madam D'Arblay), he quotes a long dedication to her diary (written at the age of fifteen); here's a segment: "to have some account of my thoughts, manners, acquaintances and actions when the hour arrives in which time is more nimble than memory is the reason which induces me to keep a journal..."

Burney began her diary at an early age. In 1774, she wrote: "I burned all up to my fifteenth birthday..." (Writing of her childhood diaries.)

When she decides to address her diary to her sister, she calls it "journalizing."

Burney had one particular faculty which can hardly have been surpassed by any other writer, and which is really the main reason that her journal gained such a wide reputation. This was her capacity for memorizing and recording conversation – not just little scraps of dialogue, but whole pages filled with conversations.

When she wrote her novel *Evelina*, she was in contact with Dr. Johnson. She concentrated her talents on recording his sayings, habits and doings in such a way that would have made Boswell very envious. In fact, Boswell asked her for "choice little notes of the Doctor" (he pleaded at length). She entered in her diary (of Boswell) that, "I evaded, declaring I had not any stories at hand... I was invincible."

2. More English Diaries From the XVIth to the XIXth Century

More English Diaries From the XVIth to the XIXth Century was compiled and edited by Arthur Ponsonby and published by Methuen & Co. Ltd., copyright 1927.

There was such a demand for more from the first volume of *English Diaries* that Mr. Ponsonby decided to do another volume on minor English diarists. He follows the same format (a list in five columns) including the name of the author, occupation, date of the diary, source and page numbers. Then he places them in chronological order: the 16th through the 19th century.

Dorothy Wordsworth was omitted from Ponsonby's first volume, which enables Ponsonby to include her diary in this volume as a "one of the best diaries by an English woman." Wordsworth could vividly describe sights and sounds of nature. She had a loving personality, which is revealed through her relationship with her brother and with the world in general.

Again, Ponsonby's commentary on the diaries he lists is what makes this a good book.

3. Scottish and Irish Diaries From the XVIth to the XIXth Century

Scottish and Irish Diaries From the XVIth to the XIXth Century was compiled by Arthur Ponsonby and published by Methuen & Co. Ltd., copyright 1927.

There is a very interesting and educational introduction to this book. Separate lists for Scottish and Irish diaries are included, and the lists are divided into five columns, as in the previously mentioned book by Ponsonby.

Ponsonby looks at fourteen separate Scottish diarists, such as diarist Marjorie Fleming. She died before her ninth birthday. He quotes her diary extensively, enough to reveal the essence of her childhood and her very unusual gift of expression.

From the Irish side, Ponsonby includes Elizabeth Freke (1671-1714) as well as ten other Irish diarists.

Elizabeth Freke comes across as a martyr in her stories of woe within her diary. She seemed to be an impossible woman; her husband left her alone and everyone quarreled with her. In six pages of diary excerpts and commentary, Ponsonby paints her life: her love for her father and of his demise, her injury from a fall, constant altercations with her husband, her husband's escape from an injury and her perception that four of her servants conspired to kill her.

Narratives

1. The Hidden Writer: Diaries and the Creative Life

The Hidden Writer: Diaries and the Creative Life was written by Alexandra A. Johnson and was published by Doubleday, copyright 1997. (Johnson currently teaches memoir at Harvard and Wellesley.)

In her prologue, Johnson tells us about diaries in general, including how diary writing came into her life. She goes on to include seven narrative portraits of the writing lives of Marjory Fleming, Sonya Tolstoy, Alice James (sister of Henry), Virginia Woolf, Katherine Mansfield, Anaïs Nin and May Sarton.

In her first chapter, *The Shadow Writer*, Johnson opens with stories about Marjory Fleming and Anne Frank. But what does she mean by "shadow writer"? She writes, "Over the centuries, many found darkly ingenious outlets for creativity. In China, knot making was perfected as an art, the knots as tight as silenced voices. In Japan, tiny pillow books were hidden under heads at night, safe from other eyes. In the Americas, poems were sealed up in convent walls or sung away as gospel hymns..."

Concerning Marjory Fleming, when she wrote in her journal in 1810, Johnson wrote: "For Twain and Stevenson, the thrill of Marjory's journal was how she'd preserved the pluck. Till the end of her short life, her words continued to surface like great bursts of oxygen."

After Marjory's death, her journals went to a friend, then to London, then to The British Museum. In 1934, they were published – over a hundred and twenty years after being written.

Anne Frank was a "shadow writer"; W W II cast a large shadow. Each night, after writing in her diary, she would hide it in her father's locked briefcase, safe from the eyes of those in the secret annex. (A hidden diary, in a hidden annex.) When the Nazis stormed in arresting all eight, Otto Frank's briefcase contents were dumped onto the floor and papers were walked on, dismissed as worthless. Miep Gies found the diary and hid it; she locked it in a drawer until Otto Frank, the only survivor of the eight, was given the diary of his daughter.

Miep Gies was one of twenty thousand Dutch people to hide Jews during the Nazi occupation of Holland. She was an employee of Anne's father. She helped all eight people hiding in the annex (as mentioned in the diary), by bringing them food and other necessities.

She found the diary after the Nazi Dutch police had raided the building and the secret annex. The diary was left on the floor. She took the red-orange checkered diary book and kept it for those who would return from the concentration camps. Only Otto Frank returned (all others perished) and she gave him the diary.

2. Leaving a Trace

Alexandra Johnson's second book, *Leaving a Trace*, was published by Little Brown, copyright 2001. In her introduction she tells the story of a diary given to her, written by a young woman who had lived in her house in 1895. The diary told a story, "with each page her life unfolded. Waiting for someone named Charlie to return from college; having her ice skates sharpened at a nearby frozen pond; going with her sister Mattie to Boston to buy sheet music..." Then she gets a job copying names from tombstones for cemetery records. Those too difficult to read had to be fingered like Braille, and others, too worn or totally gone, had vanished just like those peoples' lives and memories. "I'm sure she couldn't help wondering about those lives, just as I did about hers," writes Johnson. This story leads us nicely into the book.

"Writing," Kafka jotted in his journal, "is the axe that breaks the frozen sea within." Johnson notes that journals hint at what's long been hidden under the ice. This is part of "leaving a trace."

And she writes, "A diary is the missing link in creative life."

Johnson notes that Katherine Mansfield used her journals like small savings accounts. Mansfield wrote, "I am 33, yet I am only just beginning to see now what it is I want to do. How unbearable it would be to die – leave 'scraps,' 'bits,' nothing really finished." The journal of Katherine Mansfield has been in print ever since it was published. (She certainly has left a trace.)

This book is excellent reading for the public at large, whether you're a diarist or not.

3. Women's Diaries of the Westward Journey

Women's Diaries of the Westward Journey was written by Lillian Schlissel and was published by Schoken Books, copyright 1982.

This is a well-written, highly researched and original book. Schlissel describes some of the lives of the many people who made the journey to Oregon and California between 1841 and 1867.

The women took care of the sick and injured, made the meals, kept the children together and helped the men when needed. Many men went by themselves to the new territory and left their wives behind for years, and some never returned.

The women's diaries note that diseases – such as cholera, measles, small pox, diarrhea, malaria, scarlet fever and others – killed more of the travelers than did the Indians.

The author quotes many of the Overland women's dairy excerpts and then makes comments. Commentary and storytelling are included not just for the diaries, but also for letters, photographs (forty-eight of them), documents, statistics, maps, court documents and other primary sources (books and memoirs).

A great amount of sorrow comes through in the diary writings. Yet there is also the joyful side of those who did well and made fortunes. One might ask: "What happened to the black slaves who came to Oregon and California?" In one instance – a female slave in Los Angeles County – a Sheriff ruled that her master could not take her across the state border. This gave her freedom prior to the proclamation of 1863.

This is very good book: sensitive, historical and told in narrative with four diaries discussed, in detail, towards the end of the book.

The Illustrated Diary

The diaries mentioned in this section include illustrations, photographs, drawings, paintings, etc. These illustrations add to our education and enjoyment.

1. The Illustrated Pepys

The Illustrated Pepys contains extracts from the diary, selected and edited by Robert Latham (librarian of the Pepys Library in England) and published by the University of California Press, copyright 1978.

With fifteen color plates, numerous black and white drawings, sketches and illustrations, excerpts from the diary and comments by Mr. Latham, this book is a delight to hold, view and read.

On page 16, there's a photograph of Pepys' diary showing his handwriting and code, that is, his "made-over" version of Shelton's shorthand, a shorthand system known to the British in the 1600's.

There are black and white drawings, including: the Palace of Whitehall, King Charles II being crowned as King, Elizabeth Pepys (his wife) and many more.

Color plates include: Lady Castemaine (full page), the London fire, the London Bridge of 1660 (similar to Pontovecio in Florence Italy, today), a painting of Samuel Pepys by J. Hayles, the Dutch raid on English ships, and Whitehall from St. James Park (which is also on the dust cover).

2. Dorothy Wordsworth Illustrated – Lakeland Journals

Dorothy Wordsworth Illustrated – Lakeland Journals was published by Diamond Books, copyright 1987.

In 1800, at the age of 28, Dorothy began her personal journal and continued it to 1803. Her diary was not private, as her brother, William, read it and wrote poems from parts of it. He was inspired and almost copied her writing, including her writing of "Beggars," except he made a poem composition. The diary was published in 1897. Her reputation stands as a distinguished writer about life in the English countryside.

The book contains color prints of Dorothy, her brother William, Samuel Taylor Coleridge, Grasmere in 1800-1802, the Market Place (Ambleside), Windemere, Rydal Falls and many more. Black and white illustrations include Westminster Bridge, workers in the field, fishing in a lake, feeding chickens, a scullery maid, woodmen, a group of people reading and writing, and more.

3. Scott's Last Journey

Scott's Last Journey, edited by Peter King, was published by Harper Collins, copyright 1999.

This book not only contains Captain Scott's journal, of the race to the South Pole, written between December 1, 1910 and March 29, 1912, but also photographs, commentaries and accounts from other men on the expedition. It could have easily been named "The Illustrated Scott's Last Journey." This is because of Herbert Ponting's artistry with the camera; the book is full of his photos of the journey (1910 to 1912).

Scott's journal begins on December 1, 1910 while on stormy seas. He describes in much detail "the wind, sea, fifteen ponies stand side by side, petrol needed for sledges, cargo deck of coal and the many hands aboard."

While in the ice pack, he wrote: "December 13, we have decided to put the fire out and remain 'til conditions change."

On May 15, 1911, Scott describes his fellow workers and what they are doing: Wilson is making sketches, Simpson is working with his recording instruments, Wright is doing electrical work.

From February 19, 1912, to March 29, 1912, he writes about the struggle with winter. He knows the depot is just 11 miles away.

This is the end of Scott's last journal entry on Thursday March 29 1912:

"Every day we have been ready to start for our depot 11 miles away, but outside the door of the tent it remains a scene of whirling drift. I do not think we can hope for better things now. We shall stick it out to the end, but we are getting weaker, of course, and the end cannot be far.

It seems quite a pity, but I do not think I can write any more.

Last entry. For God's sake look after our people."

The end of the book contains farewell letters and a message to the public written by Scott. There is also an account by Lieutenant Atkinson, the expedition's surgeon, on finding the dead. This is an extract:

"Eight months afterwards the tent was found. It was an object partially snowed up and looking like a cairn."

"Inside the tent were the bodies of captain Scott, Doctor Wilson and Lieutenant Bowers. Wilson and Bowers were found in attitude of sleep, Scott died later. He had thrown the flaps of his sleeping bag and opened his coat. A little wallet containing three notebooks was under his shoulder."

4. Samuel Pepys, Esq.

Samuel Pepys, Esq. was written by Richard Barber, and was published by the University of California Press, copyright 1970. (This book is not to be confused with *The Illustrated Pepys*, selected and edited by Robert Latham.) This book is about an exhibition held in London in 1970, and about the man Samuel Pepys. In short, it is a catalogue of paintings and a list of exhibits.

There are many photographs of paintings of Samuel Pepys (probably the most famous by Hales) and some paintings of Mrs. Pepys and Lord General Monk. Other paintings include: Rump Bonfire, King departs from Scheveningen, the Royal Escape, Coronation Day, The Queen, My Lady Castemaine, Nell Gwyn, The Great Fire and more.

5. Show Your Tongue

Show Your Tongue was written by Gunter Grass and translated by John E. Woods. It was published by Harcourt Brace Jovanovich, copyright 1988.

The diary and drawings were created in India, where Gunter and his wife Ute spend six months in middle class quarters amid the crowds, noise, heat, humidity and the dirt. The diary consists of words and drawings where Gunter does not use a pen; instead, he uses a brush and brown ink.

The diary is extremely well written, including Gunter's feelings and imaginative thought.

The brush drawings of people, animals, buildings and terrain are intermingled with his writings in German. The front pages of the book are in English.

6. Out of My Mind

Out of My Mind is an autobiography written by Kristin Nelson Tinker, published by Harry N. Abrams, Inc., copyright 1977.

President Kennedy was shot and killed in November of 1963. Tinker writes about her feelings of this tragedy, of Kennedy's youth, spirit and his little children. A year after Kennedy's death, she writes: "I've been working on a painting for Mrs. Kennedy for almost a year, it's the only way I know to tell her I'm sorry."

She had never taken a painting lesson. She writes: "In 1965, I didn't send the painting, I don't know how to paint." Her husband took the painting to an art dealer. They wanted a showing of twenty of her paintings. "They are on display. After the gallery showing, almost all the paintings were sold. Then at the gallery a phone call comes from Robert Kennedy, saying 'my sister-in-law saw the painting of the White House in a newspaper article, and if still available, she would like to purchase it.'"

The book is called an autobiography because of the other work and memoranda that surround the diary: dozens of paintings, caricatures, cartoons, handwritten letters, quotes of poetry and photographs.

Tinker writes with honesty, using her own voice. Her paintings are to be seen, witnessed and felt as it's her world, published for all of us to experience.

7. The Country Diary of an Edwardian Lady
The Country Diary of an Edwardian Lady was written by Edith Holden and published by Holt, Pinehart and Winston, copyright 1977.

This is a facsimile reproduction of a naturalist's diary; it is a dairy illustrated by the author. In 1906, Holden began her diary in very neat printing. She then drew illustrations from nature: flowers, insects, butterflies, birds and their nests, snakes, bird eggs, mice, water hens, dry leaves, bramble leaves and ponds, sky, trees and starlings.

Her hand printing, extremely legible, is photographed and printed as it was written, in soft natural brown. The illustrations were printed in the same way. Only *her* art appears and no setting of type was used to publish this book.

Holden's book was a personal diary for herself and no one was allowed to see it. Seventy years later, it was found in an English country house. It was published for the first time in full color facsimile.

8. The Illustrated World of Thoreau

This book uses the words of H. D. Thoreau and photographs by Ivan Massar. It was edited by Howard Chapnick and published by Grosset and Dunlap, copyright 1974.

After a quote from Thoreau's writing, the photographer presents photographs of what Henry may have had in mind.

The written contents are mostly from Thoreau's journal as well as a few quotes from *Walden* (*Life in the Woods*).

An example is Thoreau's writings about snow crystals: "the thin snow now driving from the north and lodging on my coat consists of those beautiful star crystals, not cottony and chubby spokes...but thin and partly transparent crystals...I should hardly admire more if real stars fell and lodged on my coat. Nature is full of genius, full of divinity; so that not a snowflake escapes its fashioning hand." Following the writing is a picture of a winter scene – trees, a small cabin, and snow on the trees, in the air and on the ground. There are also three more pictures: winter flowers in fog, with snow and frost; a single plant, the lower half in snow; and another single plant with a black background, tendrils coming out of snow and its flowers and leaves with snow on their tips.

Henry writes: "To what end pray, is so much *stone hammered*? In Arcadia, when I was there I did not see any hammering stone. Nations are possessed with an insane ambition to perpetuate the memory of themselves by the amount of hammered stone they leave..."

The first picture, pertaining to the stone, is of a woman's hand holding a small stone. Then a picture (a page and a half in size) shows a workman (with a hard hat and wearing work clothes and steel-enforced shoes) standing on a group of huge boulders, leaning into a vibrating jackhammer. Another shows a large uninhabited building (of at least six stories) with smashed windows. It's made of large stone slabs, and the word "BUILDINGS" is deeply engraved in its center. Another picture is that of a rock gravestone that hasn't been chipped or broken in any way, except for the engraved words in English and Hebrew, "Thou Shalt have the Lord Thy God."

Henry writes of old age: "This old man's cheeriness was worth a thousand of the church's sacraments and *momento mori's*...It proves to me old age as tolerable, as happy, as infancy." Alongside these words is a photograph of a park scene in spring with a boy and an older man. The man is wearing a dark suit, tie, black hat, glasses and a gold chain. He's holding a black pipe and a cane. His face is thin, yet we see a smile on his face as he looks at a boy. The boy is wearing shorts and is talking to the old man; both are enjoying the moment. There's also a picture of an old woman sweeping leaves, and a separate picture of a very old black man, maybe in his late eighties, with a white beard, mustache and extra long sideburns. He wears a crocheted hat, shirt and jacket and is reading a book that he holds in his hands. He is drenched in sunshine and his white hair comes alive. There is also a photograph of a smiling mother holding her baby. The baby is reaching to kiss an old woman, its hand on her face, and the old woman is pursing her lips in anticipation.

The modern photographs in the book graphically highlight the essence of Thoreau's words, his insight into the natural world and his deep concern for humanity and the environment.

9. Letts Keep a Diary

Letts Keep a Diary, published by Charles Letts Limited, is a book of "An Exhibition of the History of Diary Keeping in Great Britain from 16th-20th Century in Commemoration of 175 years of Diary Publishing by Letts." The exhibition took place at the Mall Galleries, London, between 28 September and 25 October 1987.

This is, first, a book about the history of the Diaries of Great Britain and, secondly, a catalogue of diary books, desks, pens, ink wells, paintings, pictures, engraving and cartoons that pertain to diaries.

The book is well put together and includes many photographs of Britain's famous diarists. The book gives credit to those who hold copyrights and who lent paintings, pictures and artifacts to the exhibition. These include: Her Majesty the Queen, The Royal Academy of London, The Bodleian Library (Oxford) and the British Library (London), to name a few.

Most of the major English Diarists are included in this book, and many minor diarists as well. This includes several diarists I have not mentioned in *Window of Self*, such as: Edward VI King of England, Samuel Newton, Hester Lynch Thrale Piozzi, William Johnson, Temple (lifelong friend of Boswell), John Wesley, Capt. James Cook, William Allingham (poet), Elizabeth Barrett Browning, Thomas Carlyle (author), Charles Darwin (naturalist), Charles Dodgson (Lewis Carroll), Henry James (novelist), Frances Kemble, Beatrix Potter (writer and illustrator), John Ruskin and Beatrice Web (social reformer).

This book consists of historical writing woven with photographs, which makes it a very pleasant book.

10. The World of Louisa May Alcott

The World of Louisa May Alcott (text by William Anderson, modern photographs by David Wade) was published by Harper Perennial, copyright 1992.

The title could have been "The Illustrated Louisa May Alcott." It's a handsome book with a lot of photos, illustrations and text that animate her world. The book includes photographs and prints of Emerson, Thoreau and Hawthorne, as well as and her comments about these writers. Photographs from the Louisa

May Alcott Association are also included (from the Concord Free Public Library, and the Norman Rockwell Museum and Trust).

The book contains an illustration of the Spindle Hill Home, which her father, Bronson Alcott, sketched from memory.

Photos include the Thoreau brothers at their school, Fruitlands Museum, Wayside House, Emerson's study, Goethe, Minuteman Statue, Orchard House, sketches for Little Women, Bronson and Abba (her parents), the Old Manse, Emerson's House, Concord Bridge, Hawthorne and his study, and Thoreau (Walden House and Walden Pond).

11. The Nagle Journal

The Nagle Journal, A Diary of the Life of Jacob Nagle, Sailor, from the year 1775 to 1841, was edited by John C. Dann and published by Weidenfeld and Nicolson, copyright 1988.

In 1982, a manuscript journal by Jacob Nagle was offered at auction in a catalog by a dealer in New York City. The Clements Library at the University of Michigan was interested; that is, the director of the library, John C. Dunn, was interested. He purchased the manuscript for the library. Having a sense that the journal may not be genuine, he and his staff set out to do the work of authentication (the detective's work).

They acquired the following information, which authenticated the journal:

1. The U.S. War Department allowed a small pension for his military service and had records to prove this.
2. Pennsylvania state archives in the 19th century have his name listed as a member of the military.

3.   His found obituary notice contained a wealth of information about his family and himself.

4.   Public Records Office, National Maritime Museum at Greenwich (England) and The Indian Office Library (British Library) all show his whereabouts as a British seaman.

Many stories are told in this interesting journal, which documents the life and times of a well-traveled seaman, offering a great historical insight. Nagle was in Washington's Revolutionary Army at the age of fifteen (at the battle of the Brandywine). He then turned to the Navy (privatizing) and later was captured by the British and inscripted into the British Navy. He was with the First Fleet during Australia's settlement. He was at sea for forty-five years. He met Commander Nelson in the First French War. Nagle also sailed with the East India Company to India and China.

12. War Diary of a Combat Artist

War Diary of a Combat Artist was written and illustrated by Captain Harry Everett Townsend and edited by Alfred E. Cornebise. It is published by University Press of Colorado, copyright 1991. (Published 73 years after the last entry of the diary, which was at the and of W W I.)

Photographs and movies are not enough; they can't adequately convey the essence of combat and its effects. Only an artist can truly see beneath the surface of things and produce a work of lasting artistic value. In 1918 the U.S. Army commissioned Townsend and seven other illustrators and painters as captains in the Corps of Engineers to go to France as official combat artists. Townsend not only illustrated and photographed entire scenes, but also journalized them and recorded his activities, as well as those of his colleagues in his diary. He also recorded his talks with servicemen in the diary.

In addition to drawings and photographs, his diary recorded Big Bertha's shelling of Paris and frequent air raids of the city. He also recorded the sumptuous eating in Paris and the entertainment such as dancing ladies. With virtually unlimited travel passes, he was allowed to accompany the U.S. troops into Germany during the occupation at war's end. His diary recognized the new kind of war: tanks, aircraft and modern artillery. The combination of this observer's visual and written work makes this diary a lasting contribution to the literature of the war.

13. John Muir's Longest Walk

The full title of this book is *John Muir's Longest Walk: John Earl, a Photographer, Traces His Journey to Florida*. It was published by Doubletree & Company Inc., copyright 1975. The book includes excerpts from Muir's thousand-mile walk to the Gulf.

The photographer, John Earl, had studied Muir's travels in California, Arizona and Alaska. In this book he describes Muir's walk from Kentucky to Florida in 1867 at the age of twenty-nine. Muir kept a journal of the trip and later had it published under the title *A Thousand-Mile Walk to the Gulf*. Earl obtained a copy of the book in 1973 and he started to trace Muir's tracks (and took photographs all the way). Thus, this book includes magnificent color photographs that match Muir's steps and the words of his journal.

The first part of the book includes photographs of the Kentucky Forest and Caves (deep green forest of leaves and shadows), as well as Indian carvings, designs on rocks and the Mammoth Cave, ferns and rivers.

The entire book has breathtaking photos to accompany Muir's text.

Children's Diaries

1. A Book of One's Own

A Book of One's Own was written by Carla Stevens and published by Clarion Books, copyright 1993. This is a book for children and for teachers who teach children how to keep and write a journal. It's quite interesting, as the book quotes many children's diaries, especially those well-known. Yet it does not go into depth in any of its concepts. It does give the child and teacher ideas, but doesn't teach dialogues, observation or poetry. It just states that this can be done.

2. Julia Newberry's Diary

Julia Newberry's Diary was published by W.W. Norton and Co., Inc., copyright 1933. This diary was written by Newberry, the daughter of distinguished Chicagoan parents, between the ages of fifteen and seventeen.

The first pages of her diary show her love for the city of Chicago. She writes, "Here I am in the old house, where I was born, & where I wish I could always live; it is the dearest place on earth to me & worth all London, Paris or New York put together."

In 1871, the great Chicago fire destroyed most formal and informal documents that existed in the city at that time. Letters, diaries, journals and personal documents were lost forever. Julia was in Europe at the time of the fire and her diary was with her. Her diary is of value since it survived the fire and reveals the social climate of her time.

She danced with General Philip Sheridan aboard a U.S. warship in French waters. In 1870 she says of General Phil Sheridan, the hero of the recent war: "We had a dashing call from Gen. Phil. Sheridan the other night; he is distingué, but frightfully ugly. (perhaps not frightfully but still anything but handsome.) He is very short, (shorter than I.) very broad; & his eyes are only long narrow holes..."

When she first heard and saw Johann Strauss, she wrote that he "acted like a monkey." However, in another occasion (at a ball), she wrote, "when Strauss led, it was perfectly magnificent; he inspires the band to such a degree, that they play as if under enchantment;...Strauss is beyond anything I ever imagined..."

3. Hawthorne's First Diary

Hawthorne's First Diary, With an Account of its Discovery and Loss was written by Samuel T. Pickard and published by Houghton, Mifflin and Company, copyright 1897.

Nathaniel's father died when he was quite young. At the age of nine, he went with his mother to live in Raymond, Maine. There he lived a life all boys anywhere would want. He was given a sack lunch, and with his fishing pole and fowling piece he was off by himself for the entire day. At that time, the area of Raymond, Maine, was mainly primeval forests, lakes and streams. He would find other boys and old men who were fishing and hunting. Thus, he was free, as nature intended. Here in Raymond he started diary writing and continued throughout his life.

A few extracts:

"Yesterday in a sailboat on the Great Pond with Mr. Peter White..."

"Swapped pocket knives with Robinson Cook yesterday. Jacob Dingley says he cheated me; but I think not, for I cut a fishing pole this morning, and did it well. Besides, he is a Quaker, and they never cheat."

Within the book is the story of William Symmes. Symmes, a boyhood friend of Hawthorne, had moved from Maine to West Virginia. During the Civil War, he was friendly with some union troops, one from the Raymond area. This soldier told Symmes that he helped Hawthorne's mother move a lot of furniture; in a bookcase, he found a journal; it might have been Nathaniel's. Symmes stated that he was a true friend of Hawthorne's – had gone fishing and hunting with him as a boy in Raymond, and further stated that he would be very happy to have the journal. The soldier said that he'd save it and would send it to him after the end of the war, if he lived through it. And so he did. Symmes never showed the book to anyone. Instead, he sent extracts from the boyhood diary from time to time to the local newspaper in Raymond. He never gave a return address and only used his initials. The paper and the book publisher checked it all out and believed Symmes had the true manuscript diary.

Symmes described the diary to the newspaper as, "originally a bound blank one, not ruled, been chewed by mice or eaten by moths on the edges." On the first leaf, in a beautiful round hand, is written the following:

"Presented by Richard Manning, to his nephew Nathaniel Hawthorne, with the advice that he write out his thoughts, some every day, in as good words as he can, upon any and all subjects, as it is one of the best means of his securing for mature years, command of thoughts and language.

Raymond, June 1, 1816."

4. 1880-1884 Mary Scarborough Paxson, Her Book

1880-1884 Mary Scarborough Paxson, Her Book was published by Doubleday, Dolan & Co Inc., copyright 1932.

This is one of the most delightfully written diaries by a child. Mary was only seven (she tells us so and a lot more) when she writes:

"*January, 15 1880* I got laughed at in school today and dident like it, the teacher asked me what is the smallest fur berring animal and I said a catterpiller and I ought to say a mouse and I don't care a catterpiller is littler than a mouse and it has fur on it,"

"*February, 7 1880,* I wouldent know how to spell the Months if I dident copy it out of the callender, Marrie and I went to the librerry and we got little women to read we love the books that Louisa Alcott makes and Mamma is going to read it to us while we hem a towel and sew our patch work, I made my doll a pretty cot this morning, when I am grone up I am going to make books like Louisa Alcott does"

"*March 21,1880,* I let a little mouse out of the trap today nobody saw me do it,"

The entire book is filled with such gems.

5. Theodore Roosevelt's diaries of Boyhood and Youth

Theodore Roosevelt's diaries of Boyhood and Youth was published by Charles Scribner's and Sons, New York, copyright 1928.

In 1868, Teddy is nine years of age and begins his diary. Then, in 1869 to 1870, he and his family traveled in Europe. Visiting many places, this young lad tells us what he sees, about his illness (asthma), and what he feels and what he's interested in. They travel the British Isles and the parts of the Grand Tour of Europe.

Among the many recordings of this ten-year-old are: "visited residence of Sir Walter Scott, the down Lock Katrine (where the poem *Lady of the Lake* was written). I drew a plan of a lost boat." In London, he and his sisters go to the zoological gardens several times in the course of a week. "We had a splendid romp in Hyde Park." "Went to British Museum, (a couple of times)." "We 3 went to the Crystal Palace again." He is very interested in birds and reptiles.

He treks from country to country. In Holland, at the Museum at The Hague, he writes: "We saw many Chinese weapons, crockery and models."

This boy is getting quite an education, along with the help of his caring family. From this boyhood and youth diary we learn about his likes, how a boy acts and plays, his particular characteristics and habits, and the spirit of Teddy Roosevelt as he is growing up.

6. The Diary of "Helena Morley" (Minha Vida de Menina)

The Diary of "Helena Morley" was translated and edited by Elizabeth Bishop, published by The Ecco Press, copyright 1957.

Minha Vida de Menina, literally translated, means "My life as a Young Girl." There are many wonderful stories written by Helena (between age twelve and fifteen) during the years 1893 and 1895 in a far away town of Diamantia, Brazil.

The town of Diamantia is in a remote area of high elevation. A river runs through it and there is much vegetation there. The town is named for the many diamond mines that existed there in the mid-1800's.

Some excerpts:
"January 5, 1893. Today is the best day of the week. On Thursdays (school holiday) Mama wakes up at daybreak... We go down the lane, which is very narrow, and came out on the bridge. It's the best spot in Diamantia and it's always deserted. We never meet anyone there, that's why Mama chose it.

"Mama sends for Emídio from the *chácara* (a house with small garden) and puts the big tin basin of laundry on top of his head, and the ball of soft soap on top of that. Renato takes pots and pans and things to eat in the little cart and we start off. Mama, Luizinha, and I go down under the bridge to wash the clothes. Emídio goes to look for firewood. Renato fishes for *lambaris* (tiny fish); I never saw as many as there are there. He just has to put on the bait, drop in the hook, and he immediately pulls out either a *lambari* or a shad. Nhonhô spreads birdlime on a twig and stays a little way off watching for birds. When he catches one he runs out and cleans off the poor little thing's feet with oil and puts it in the cage. Then he puts more birdlime on the twigs and after a little while another bird arrives, a linnet, or a sparrow.

"We to wash the clothes and spread them out to bleach and then mama makes our lunch, *tutu* (small balls of black beans) with rice and pork cracklings.

"After we've finished washing the clothes and eating our lunch, mama keeps a lookout on the road to see if anyone is coming and we got in the river to take baths and wash our hair.

"After that we beat the clothes on the stones and rinse them and hang them on bushes to dry. Then we can go to look for berries and bird's nests and cocoons, and little round stones to play jackstones with…

"Now that the mines aren't producing diamonds any bigger than a mosquito's eye, what a big saving it would make for mama if we could go to the bridge every day, because Renato and Nhonhô sell everything they bring back on the same day."

"Saturday January 21, 1893. The thing that all of us, the boys and girls of Boa Vista, like to do best is, after we've had dinner and papa and Uncle Joãozinho have dismissed the workmen, to climb up and down the waste of the mine in our bare feet, in the mud, looking for little diamonds and flakes of gold, because my uncle will buy them all. We hardly ever find a diamond but we always find flakes of gold.

"We were all, all the children, going from one side to the other with our eyes fixed on the waste. Arinda was with us. All of a sudden she screamed and bent down and picked up a really big diamond. We all ran to the house to get papa and my uncle. He looked at it and said to papa, "Look, Alexandre, what a beautiful stone!" and gave Arinda five brand-new hundred *mil reis* notes." (She took it to her poor father, who gave her nothing in return and would gamble it on an abandoned mine.)

Helena later married, had children and grandchildren, and lived in Rio in grand style. She stated that the happiest days of her life were at Diamantia – before the automobile and motion pictures.

The editor, Elizabeth Bishop, says (in the introduction) that the diary reminded her of Dorothy Wordworth's *Wandering Beggars*, and that the slaves seemed like notes of a feminine version of Tom Sawyer and Nigger Joe. However, this was a child's day-by-day writing; not a story told by an adult.

7. The Diary of The Vilna Ghetto

The Diary of The Vilna Ghetto was written by Yitskhok Rudashevski and published by Hakibbutz Hameuchad Publishing House, and Ghetto Fighter's House, Israel. It's translated from the original Yiddish manuscript by Percy Matenko.

My wife Helen and I visited the Ghetto Fighter's House, near Hefa, Israel in 1988. It is a holocaust museum, similar to the one in Washington D.C. I noticed large maps drawn on the walls depicting various concentration camps of the Nazis. One, to my surprise, was that of Gunskirken Lager in Austria. My thoughts immediately went back to 1945 when I was in Patton's 3rd Army, 77th Division, and was the first to reach the camp and to break the gates. Eighteen thousand people were there, being starved to death.

As we were about to leave the Ghetto Fighter's Museum, I found Rudashevski's diary.

The diary was written from June 1941 to April 1943. It contrasts with Anne Frank's diary in one major way: Anne writes about those in confinement with her; Yitskhok writes about an entire village.

He begins his diary when the German army takes over the Ghetto (Webster defines "Ghetto" as the quarters of a city to which Jews were restricted for residence). He is fourteen years of age. He was a serious and diligent student, and he probed deeply into whatever he studied. He belonged to literature, history and natural science clubs. In one entry of the diary, he writes: "because I consider that everything should be recorded and written down, even the most gory, everything will be taken into account."

Thus, Yitskhok wrote of the psychological and actual brutal force of the Nazi's on his people: "Long lines for food (bread and other products), Germans go into the rooms and throw out the Jews." "Our life is a life of helpless terror." "The decree was issued that we put on badges front and back, a yellow circle and inside the letter J."

Some were issued red certificates, others white and some pink. (Red meant you had work and then you were not killed.)

Ponar was a place (about eight miles from Vilna) where they were sent in groups to be shot dead and then burned on fires. Of the thousands in the Vilna Ghetto, all were sent to Ponar, to perish, except one young woman.

This young woman was being marched to Ponar (with others), but when the German guards were not looking, she ran into the woods and escaped. Later she went to the ghetto and, on a pile of rubble, found Yitskhok's hand-written diary. It found its way to Israel where it was published.

The diary is one of the strongest documents depicting German brutality and the insane belief in the final solution.

In Conclusion

Diary books have enormous value. Diary writing is one person writing what he believes to be important at the time. It's recorded for himself, to be looked at later, or to be used later by others. We learn from diaries of the Revolutionary War, by the minds and pens of those on each side of the conflict. There are many of them and if you want to get into the minds of these persons it can be done.

Major libraries and university libraries are the true source for published and manuscript diaries. If they do not have what you want, they can find it. It is also to be noted, the Internet is a place to do your hunting.